Bilbao

COS DE EUROPA

PYRENEES

PICO DE ANETO

Ter

Llobregat

SIERRA DE GUADARRAMA

Ebro

MONTSERRAT

Segre

Barcelona

ERA CENTRAL

REDOS • Madrid

• Toledo

S DE TOLEDO

Valencia

SIERRA DE ALCARAZ

Segura

BALEARIC ISLANDS

CORDILLERA BÉTICA

MULHACÉN

SIERRA NEVADA

Melilla

N

SPAIN

SPAIN

By the Editors of Time-Life Books

TIME-LIFE BOOKS ∘ ALEXANDRIA, VIRGINIA

TIME LIFE BOOKS ®

Other Publications:

FIX IT YOURSELF
FITNESS, HEALTH & NUTRITION
SUCCESSFUL PARENTING
HEALTHY HOME COOKING
UNDERSTANDING COMPUTERS
THE ENCHANTED WORLD
THE KODAK LIBRARY OF
 CREATIVE PHOTOGRAPHY
GREAT MEALS IN MINUTES
THE CIVIL WAR
PLANET EARTH
COLLECTOR'S LIBRARY OF THE CIVIL WAR
THE EPIC OF FLIGHT
THE GOOD COOK
WORLD WAR II
HOME REPAIR AND IMPROVEMENT
THE OLD WEST

This volume is one in a series of books describing countries of the world — their natural resources, peoples, histories, economies and governments.

For information on and a full description of any of the Time-Life Books series listed above, please write:
Reader Information
Time-Life Books
541 North Fairbanks Court
Chicago, Illinois 60611

Time-Life Books Inc.
is a wholly owned subsidiary of

TIME INCORPORATED

FOUNDER: Henry R. Luce 1898-1967

Editor-in-Chief: Henry Anatole Grunwald
Chairman and Chief Executive Officer: J. Richard Munro
President and Chief Operating Officer: N. J. Nicholas Jr.
Chairman of the Executive Committee: Ralph P. Davidson
Corporate Editor: Ray Cave
Executive Vice President, Books: Kelso F. Sutton
Vice President, Books: George Artandi

TIME-LIFE BOOKS INC.

EUROPEAN EDITOR: Kit van Tulleken
Assistant European Editor: Gillian Moore
Design Director: Ed Skyner
Photography Director: Pamela Marke
Chief of Research: Vanessa Kramer
Chief Sub-editor: Ilse Gray

LIBRARY OF NATIONS

Series Editor: Ellen Galford

Editorial Staff for *Spain*
Editor: Tony Allan
Researcher: Krystyna Mayer
Designer: Lynne Brown
Sub-editors: Wendy Gibbons, Sally Rowland
Picture Department: Christine Hinze, Peggy Tout
Editorial Assistant: Molly Oates

EDITORIAL PRODUCTION
Production Assistants: Nikki Allen, Alan Godwin, Maureen Kelly
Editorial Department: Theresa John, Debra Lelliott

Valuable help was given in the preparation of this volume by Berta Julia (Barcelona), Maria Vincenza Aloisi (Paris) and Trini Bandres (Madrid).

Contributors: The chapter texts were written by: Douglas Botting, John Cottrell, Robert Graham, Frederic V. Grunfeld and Alan Lothian.

Assistant Editor for the U.S. edition: Barbara Fairchild Quarmby

CONSULTANTS

Professor Raymond Carr, Warden of St. Antony's College, Oxford, England, has written many books and articles on Spanish history, including *Spain 1808-1939*, *Spain: Dictatorship to Democracy* and *Modern Spain*.

Sheelagh Ellwood, a historian attached to the Center for Contemporary Spanish Studies at the University of London's Queen Mary College, lives in Madrid.

First printing.
Printed in U.S.A.
Published simultaneously in Canada.
School and library distribution by Silver Burdett Company, Morristown, New Jersey.

TIME-LIFE is a trademark of Time Incorporated U.S.A.

Library of Congress Cataloguing in Publication Data
Spain.
 (Library of nations)
 Bibliography: p.
 Includes index.
 1. Spain. I. Time-Life Books. II. Series.
DP17.S63 1987   946   87-1922
ISBN 0-8094-5181-6
ISBN 0-8094-5182-4 (lib. bdg.)

Cover: Near the castle of Consuegra in the province of Toledo, whitewashed windmills stand guard on an exposed ridge. The buildings, some of them dating back to the 16th century, recall those that Don Quixote attacked in Miguel de Cervantes' classic novel.

Pages 1 and 2: On page 1, the State Coat of Arms unites the crests of Castile, Leon, Aragon and Navarre under the royal crown. The coat of arms is displayed on Spain's national flag, shown on page 2.

Front and back endpapers: A topographic map showing the major rivers, mountain ranges and other natural features of Spain appears on the front endpaper; the back endpaper shows the 17 Autonomous Communities, or principal regions, and the main towns.

CONTENTS

Near the village of Capileira in the Sierra Nevada region of Andalusia, a farmer plows a stubbly hillside behind a team of oxen. By 1970, Spain's rural

A MOVEMENT FROM THE SOIL

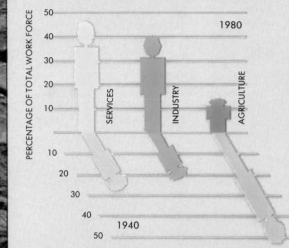

PERCENTAGE OF TOTAL WORK FORCE

50 40 30 20 10 10 20 30 40 50

1980

1940

SERVICES

INDUSTRY

AGRICULTURE

Over the last 50 years, Spain's work force has shifted dramatically from agricultural to industrial employment. At the end of the Civil War in 1939, more than half the population worked on the land, often in bitter poverty as subsistence farmers or day laborers. In the following decades, the industrial sector grew, and hundreds of thousands of peasants abandoned the countryside for factory jobs in the major cities — Barcelona and Madrid — or to work abroad. Meanwhile, employment opportunities grew in such areas as banking, retailing and government administration. By 1984, with mechanization further reducing farming's labor needs, agriculture employed only 14.4 percent of the country's working population.

exodus had drained the region of 1.6 million of its inhabitants; nearly half of those migrants resettled in Barcelona.

A TRIO OF CLIMATIC ZONES

From its Atlantic coast to its Mediterranean shore, Spain straddles three distinct climatic zones, each suited to different agricultural methods and products. The humid, maritime climate of the northwest provides Spain's only pasture and forest land. In addition to raising beef and dairy cattle, farmers there cultivate corn, apples and pears.

A Mediterranean climate with hot, dry summers and cool, rainy winters prevails in a zone that stretches along the southeastern coast and curves inland up the Ebro valley in the north.

The major crops of this area are deep-rooted olive trees and grapevines, plants that can tap subterranean ground water. Citrus and other fruits also thrive, while industrial crops, such as cotton, hemp and tobacco, are a secondary source of income.

Spain's interior, the Meseta plateau, is a region of semiarid steppe. It produces the country's chief grain crops: wheat in the better-watered and more fertile western interior and barley in the drier south. Millions of sheep and goats graze the uncultivated areas of the plateau.

A yellow carpet of sunflowers, grown for their oil, stretches to the Andalusian horizon. With limited dairy farming, Spain depends largely on vegetable

oil for fat. Of the country's industrial-crop production, sunflower oil is second only to olive oil in volume.

THE CHURCH ON THE DEFENSIVE

In recent years, Spanish Catholicism has experienced a decline both in its institutional power and its popular support. Its historic position of privilege as the religion of Spain's kings was reinforced under General Franco, whose cause the Church had supported during the Civil War. The 1962 Vatican Council rejected this close identification with the dictatorship and endorsed separation of church and state. Spain's 1978 constitution formally dissolved the relationship, while acknowledging the Church's moral force in society. But that force is diminishing: Although 95 percent of the population is nominally Catholic, only 20 percent of city dwellers regularly attend Mass.

In Seville, scarlet-robed priests and bishops lead a Palm Sunday procession carrying sun-bleached fronds from Spain's Elche forest, the largest palm

plantation in Europe. After receiving a traditional blessing, the palms, which are sold throughout Spain, bedeck the balconies of worshippers.

11

CENTERS OF POPULATION

Spain's population has risen rapidly in the last century, with its yearly growth rate climbing from 0.34 percent in 1860 to 1.15 percent in 1981. Despite a drop in that annual rate during the years of hardship following the Civil War, the population has more than doubled, from 16,632,000 in the 1870s to an estimated 38,997,458 in 1984. Approximately one quarter of Spain's people live either in Madrid, the nation's capital, or in Barcelona, chief city of the northeastern region of Catalonia. Those cities and their surrounding areas — together with the Basque Country, the Canary Islands and the Balearic Islands — are the most densely inhabited areas of Spain. The large interior region of Castile-La Mancha has the sparsest population: Its density of 52 people per square mile is about the same as Iowa's or Minnesota's.

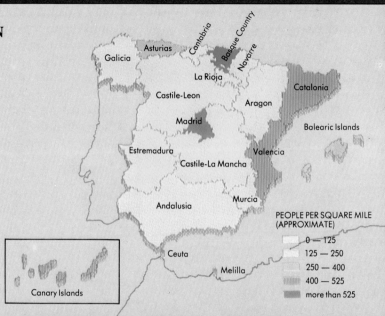

PEOPLE PER SQUARE MILE
(APPROXIMATE)

- 0 — 125
- 125 — 250
- 250 — 400
- 400 — 525
- more than 525

Beneath a lowering sky, the whitewashed houses of a walled town follow the contours of the Andalusian hills. Spain's largest region, Andalusia is home

to nearly 18 percent of the nation's inhabitants, but its population density is only 190 people per square mile.

A BOOM IN TOURISM

VISITORS (MEASURED IN MILLIONS)

40
30
20
10

1955 1960 1965 1970 1975 1980

Despite temporary downturns in the early and the late 1970s, when worldwide oil crises kept many travelers at home, tourism has been one of the main growth industries in Spain for more than 30 years. Between the mid-1950s and the mid-1980s, the annual number of visitors to Spain rose fifteenfold. And beginning in the mid-1970s, the country welcomed more foreigners each year than there were native-born Spaniards: France and Portugal provided the greatest number of visitors, followed by Britain and West Germany. Besides making a vital contribution to Spain's balance of payments, the tourist boom has generated growth in several industries, particularly transportation and construction. In resort areas, it has led to improvements in public services, such as health care, communications and utilities.

Winding across the black lava soil of Lanzarote in the Canary Islands, a convoy of camels carries sightseers to the Montaña de Fuego, volcanic cones that

testify to the island's violent birth. With three million visitors a year, the Canary Islands are Spain's second most popular tourist region.

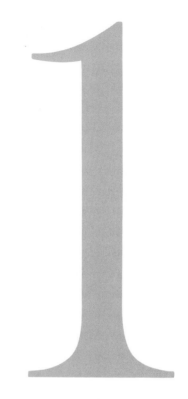

The ancient city of Toledo, dominated
by its single-spired Gothic cathedral
and the turreted fortress of the Alcázar,
rises above the Tagus River in central
Spain. As the capital of the country until 1561, Toledo was a center of learning and the arts that fused Moorish,
Jewish and Christian cultures.

A MAJESTIC LAND SET APART

The high, square mass of the Iberian Peninsula, of which Spain occupies by far the greatest area — 194,897 square miles, or nearly five sixths of the whole — is so cut off by the solid barrier of the Pyrenees and reaches so far westward into the Atlantic that it seems almost an island. "A fragment nipped off from hot Africa, soldered so crudely to inventive Europe," is how the poet W. H. Auden described it. Certainly much of Spain bears a physical resemblance to northern Africa. But Spain also holds a strategic position dividing two expanses of water — the Atlantic and the Mediterranean — and two continental land masses: Africa and Europe proper. This gives the country a richly hybrid character and has been one reason for Spain's critical importance in the past and for the many wars that have been waged across its soil.

Two other geographical factors have had a crucial bearing on Spain's history and continue to shape its development: its relief and its climate. Spain has the highest mean altitude of any country in Europe after Switzerland. A large portion of the country, totaling some 40 percent of the land mass, is a tableland of windswept, nearly treeless steppe known as the Meseta, which rises to a mean elevation of 1,970 feet. Great mountain ranges hem in this inland plateau — the Pyrenees and the Cantabrians to the north, the Andalusian mountains of the Sierra Nevada to the south. Ten other mountain ranges traverse the interior, notably the 435-mile-long sierras of the Guadarrama range and the Gredos mountains.

Natural routes through these inhospitable uplands are few and far between. The coastal plains are narrow and constricted and cut off from the interior. Spanish rivers, it has been said, possess "a long name, a narrow channel and little water." The majority of them are unnavigable — as dry as an arroyo in the American southwest for most of the year and raging torrents for the brief season of spring rain. Of the great rivers of Spain — the Ebro, Duero, Tajo, Guadiana and Guadalquivir — the last is the only useful waterway, and Seville on its banks is the only major river port.

The rugged terrain of so much of Spain has long been a barrier to communications between the different parts of the country, especially between the coast and the interior and between the north and the south. For centuries, Spain was divided up into regions so isolated from one another that the Spanish monarch was once known not as the King of Spain but as King of the Spains. It was a centrifugal land, with most of its important regions spread out along the periphery.

Until recently, these regions, each of them highly individualistic, have traditionally looked to the outside world for trade and contact rather than to the ruling center in Castile. To the north, Galicia and the Basque lands have

1

turned to the Atlantic and northern Europe for their wealth; Catalonia and Valencia in the east focus their attention on the Mediterranean, Italy and Provence; Andalusia in the south leans to Africa and the Americas. Thus the possibility has always existed that the peninsula might fragment into a number of independent states — although only Portugal, in 1640, ever achieved permanent separation from Spain.

The lack of a historic capital like London or Paris delayed for centuries a centripetal unity of the kind enjoyed by England or France. Many towns in Spain were used as administrative centers before King Philip II made Madrid the capital in the late 16th century. But for many years, Madrid was an artificial creation, and until the industrial revolution of the 1960s, it was without large-scale resources of its own. "Everyone works for Madrid," went the saying, "and Madrid works for no one." It never succeeded in welding Spain into a nation as Paris had welded France.

Spain's inherent regionalism is accentuated by its climate, which has created such marked differences in vegetation, agriculture and way of life that different areas of the country look as if they belong to utterly separate lands. The north coast has a climate similar in many respects to Oregon's, with frequent rain, thick mists and abundant dew. Its greenness and lushness are in startling contrast to the drier, hotter, subtropical areas of the Mediterranean littoral in the south and east, and to the continental extremes of temperature in the central tableland of the Meseta. There, summer burns and winter freezes; little rain falls in any season, and the land is parched and dry for months and even years on end. Almost one quarter of Spain — mainly in the

southeast — is classed as "arid," with less than 16 inches of rain a year. Near Cabo de Gata in Almería, where the annual rainfall is four and a half inches, lies Europe's only true desert.

The aridity of so much of the country is reflected in the barren and treeless landscapes of the interior, the 200 days of cloudless skies in every Andalusian year and the clarity of the night sky, which lights up the landscape with remarkable brilliance. Violent extremes of temperature occur over much of the Meseta, where it is said the climate consists of *tres meses de invierno y nueve de infierno* — three months of winter and nine of hell. In Madrid in summer, the shady side of the street may be 15 degrees cooler than the sunny side, the night 25 degrees cooler than the day and the coldest winter day (10° F.) 100 degrees cooler than the hottest summer

day (110° F.). The summers in the capital are so hot and dry that the city's waterways shrivel to puddles; yet in an exceptional winter, it may be so cold that it is possible to go ice skating along them. The biting raw wind of Madrid is so subtle, the proverb goes, *"que mata a un hombre, y no apaga un candil"* — "it will kill a man, but not blow out a candle."

In the wet north, there are high mountains, woods and forests of oak, beech, larch, ash and chestnut, green meadows and fat cows in forest clearings, orchards of apples and fields of grain, neat little villages of Swiss-style chalets and trout streams rushing under Roman bridges. Farther south, where the typical trees of arid Spain are the pines (Aleppo, cluster, stone, Corsican), the oaks (cork, evergreen), Spanish fir and incense juniper, the harsh climate and the ravages of men and goats have all but eliminated continuous woodland. In its place, large tracts have been sown with grain and pasture or are overgrown by the *monte bajo,* or *matorral:* low, scrubby aromatic or spiny bushes such as thyme, rosemary, lavender, gorse and stunted oaks, often covering enormous areas in impenetrable thickets that were once a favorite refuge of bandits.

In the semidesert steppes of La Mancha, the plant cover has degenerated into dry, tufted grasses and wormwood, which cannot hide the desolate expanse of bare soil. By contrast, the more favored areas of the Mediterranean coastlands and the plain of Andalusia make up a region of vineyards, olive woods and orange groves and — in the green gardens of the irrigated oases, called *huertas,* or *vegas* — tropical produce including bananas, rice, sugar and cotton, melons, figs, pomegranates and jujube abounds. Alicante, like

A SYSTEM OF SELF-GOVERNING REGIONS

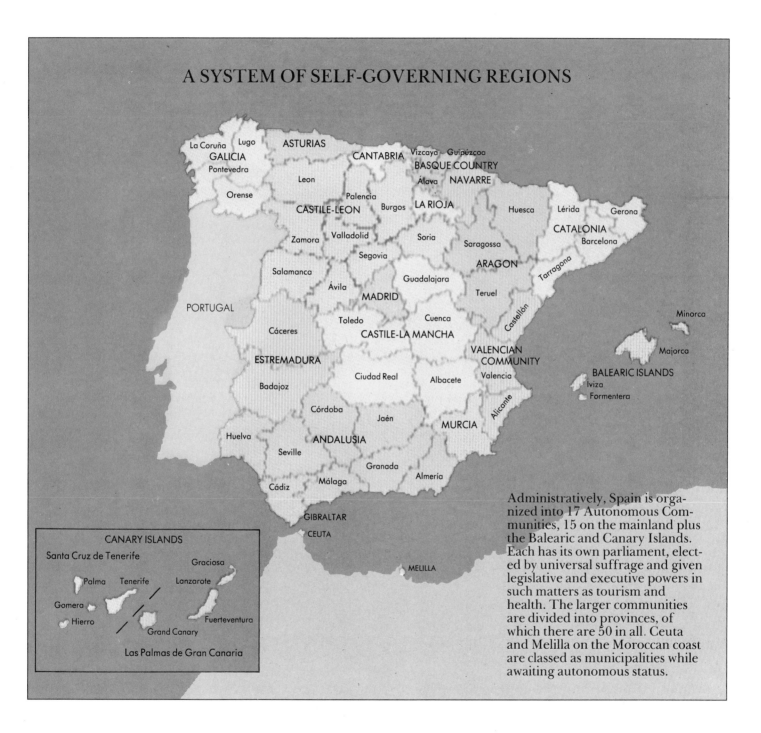

La Coruña Lugo
GALICIA
Pontevedra
Orense

ASTURIAS

CANTABRIA
Vizcaya Guipúzcoa
BASQUE COUNTRY
Álava NAVARRE

Leon

Palencia
CASTILE-LEON Burgos LA RIOJA
Zamora Valladolid Soria
Segovia
Salamanca
Ávila
MADRID

Huesca Lérida Gerona
CATALONIA Barcelona

Saragossa
ARAGON Tarragona
Teruel
Guadalajara
Castellón

PORTUGAL

Cáceres
Toledo Cuenca
CASTILE-LA MANCHA

ESTREMADURA

Badajoz
Ciudad Real Albacete

VALENCIAN
COMMUNITY
Valencia

Minorca
Majorca
BALEARIC ISLANDS
Iviza
Formentera

Córdoba
Jaén
Huelva
Seville ANDALUSIA
Granada Almería
Cádiz Málaga
MURCIA
Alicante

GIBRALTAR
CEUTA

MELILLA

Administratively, Spain is organized into 17 Autonomous Communities, 15 on the mainland plus
the Balearic and Canary Islands.
Each has its own parliament, elected by universal suffrage and given
legislative and executive powers in
such matters as tourism and
health. The larger communities
are divided into provinces, of
which there are 50 in all. Ceuta
and Melilla on the Moroccan coast
are classed as municipalities while
awaiting autonomous status.

CANARY ISLANDS
Santa Cruz de Tenerife
Graciosa
Palma Tenerife Lanzarote
Gomera
Hierro Fuerteventura
Grand Canary
Las Palmas de Gran Canaria

some African seaside resort, is a city of palms. Seville, a few hours' drive from the permanent snows of the high Sierra Nevada, is hot enough to grow avocados — and some of the best and biggest olives in the world.

These differences in climate and cultivation have inspired Spain's richly varied regional cookery. In Málaga, source of the best muscat raisins, the abundant grapes are combined with garlic and almonds in a chilled grape soup. In Asturias, a warming broadbean and smoked-sausage stew called *fabada* provides an antidote to the long and rainy winters. Castilians roast lamb and suckling pig on spits. In sunny Andalusia, ripe tomatoes, peppers and other vegetables are made into a cold vegetable soup, the so-called liquid salad known as gazpacho. Mahón, Minorca, is said to be the home of the salad dressing known everywhere as mayonnaise; Catalonia brought forth the fiery pepper sauce called *romesco*. The beverages that wash down these specialties are equally varied. In the northwest, people quaff cider and the young, green wine called *riberio*. At the annual festivals in the south, revelers sip ice-cold half-bottles of fortified aromatic wines called sherry, Montilla or Malaga (a kind of Andalusian Marsala). And in Madrid, they slake their thirst with *horchata*, a soft drink made from the tiger nuts grown around Valencia.

The people of the different regions of Spain are as disparate as its weather and landscape. They are the descendants of successive waves of immigrants: Iberians from North Africa; Nordic hunters and Celts from across the Pyrenees; Phoenician, Carthaginian and Greek settlers; Roman colonists; Visigoths from Germany; Jews of the Diaspora; and, not least, Muslim Moors from North Africa, who ruled parts of the peninsula for almost eight centuries and made an indelible impression on the character of Spain.

The diverse origins of the Spanish people can be heard as well as seen. Although pure Castilian — the language of Madrid and the Meseta, and the official form of Spanish since 1230 — is spoken as a first language by 75 percent of the population, the rest have their own native tongues. Fifty thousand people speak Basque; in the northwestern region of Galicia, the local population speaks Gallego, a form of Portuguese; and in Catalonia to the northeast, they speak Catalan, a Latin-derived language with similarities to Italian and Provençal as well as Spanish. In remoter regions, even Castilian exists in dialects that are incomprehensible to the untutored ear: Montares in the Cantabrian mountains, Hecho and Anso in the high valleys of the Pyrenees, Extremeño in Estremadura, and Andalusian dialects of heavy, unusual accent and rich vocabulary so highly localized that words used in one village are replaced by an entirely different set of words in another.

As every ruler of Spain has been aware, local dissimilarities can all too easily turn into political divisiveness. During the dictatorial 36-year rule of General Francisco Franco, victor in the brutal Civil War that rent the nation in

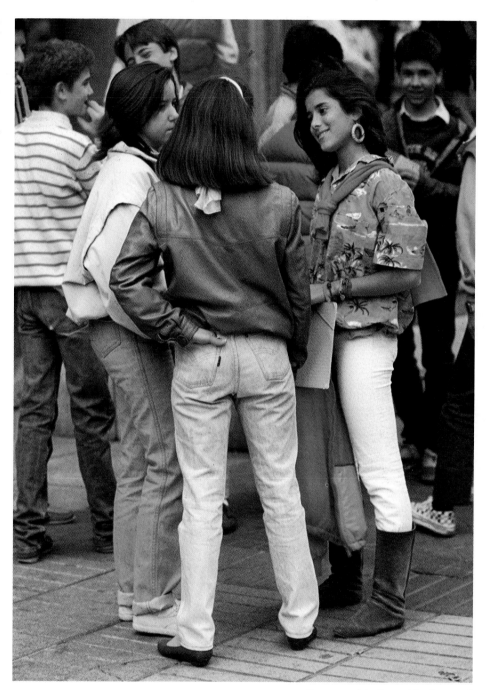

Teen-age girls dressed in the casual style of their counterparts throughout Europe exchange gossip outside a Madrid school. Liberalized social mores, fostered by the arrival of democracy, have brought an independence to single Spanish women that was unheard of in the 1950s.

the 1930s, concern over regionalism became an obsession. Using every means in his power, Franco sought to impose unity by decreeing uniformity. Decisions emanated from Madrid; every manifestation of local independence was regarded with suspicion.

Not the least of the great changes that have affected the country since Franco's death in 1975 — and the restoration of parliamentary democracy under a constitutional monarch — has been a total reversal of the official policy of centralization. Now devolution is the watchword, and for purposes of local administration, the country has been divided into 17 regions — the Autonomous Communities — each with a single-chamber Parliament.

In the extreme northwest of Iberia lies Galicia, a region very different from the Spain of the travel brochures. Its wild granite shores and sea lochs, its west Atlantic winds, its clammy hanging mists, its green hills and valleys, its stone-walled fields and slate roofs weighted down against the winter storms are reminiscent of Ireland, Brittany or the west coast of Scotland. Appropriately, the Galicians are themselves of Celtic origin — the name derives from the same semantic root as Gaelic, Gaul and Wales — and they still play the bagpipes. This is the base for much of Spain's fishing industry, and the comparative absence of frost and the abundance of rain make it a good agricultural territory too. Every square foot of the tiny fields and manmade terraces cut into the hillsides is under intensive cultivation, growing a wide variety of crops — corn, potatoes, tomatoes, rye, beans, as well as lemons and grapes. The high ground that cannot be farmed is verdant with wild vegeta-

Drowsy from the heat, a man in an Andalusian town rubs his eyes after his siesta — an afternoon rest during the hottest part of the day. Less popular in the north, the siesta is still a common practice in southern Spain, where midday temperatures are frequently higher than 95° F.

tion—thick broom, gorse, ferns, chestnuts, oaks and pines. Twenty-five percent of Spain's timber comes from here. This is green Spain, intensively worked and densely populated.

Although Galicia is populous, it is not prosperous. Galicia is above all a land of *minifundias*—small farms. "Gallegans do not use handkerchiefs," the locals joke, "they till them." Farmland is divided into minute, fragmented strips the size of small gardens clustered around little settlements with populations that are generally less than 200. "Behind each hedge, there is a Gallego," runs a Galician proverb; "behind each rock, a house."

The uneconomic subdivision of the land into tiny plots, too small to be developed efficiently, has been one of the reasons that Galician agriculture, although it has productive potential, has always hovered near the subsistence level. Another reason has been the region's remote position and poor communications with the rest of the country; indeed, it was long administered more like a colony than a province.

But great changes are under way. A program of road building, including the construction of a major new highway, will link the region's main cities with the rest of Spain. Along the coast, the small towns and fishing ports have already experienced an unprecedented population growth. Galicians who once sought opportunity elsewhere are returning in droves. As a consequence, parts of the shoreline are beginning to resemble rural cities of the kind seen in Southeast Asia, where tall buildings loom over tiny plots of beans and corn. Galicia is now the victim of uncontrolled market forces. Local smugglers (responsible for most of the foreign tobacco consumed in Spain) have invested their ill-gotten gains in construction and in land speculation. And the boom threatens to destroy one of Galicia's greatest assets, its beauty.

Between Galicia and the Pyrenees stretch the 6,560-foot ramparts of the Cantabrian Cordillera. Running parallel to Spain's Atlantic coast and looking northward across the Bay of Biscay, this rugged barrier of snow-capped peaks, fast-flowing water, gorges and forested slopes proved too much for the otherwise all-conquering Moors; as a result, Asturias, Galicia's green and prosperous neighbor, remained a bastion of Spanish resistance throughout the Muslim occupation.

Modern-day Asturias, in conjunction with the contiguous region of Cantabria, is one of the most important industrial areas in Spain. The mines south of Oviedo provide 70 percent of all Spain's pit coal and 15 percent of its anthracite, and coal production has given rise to one of the greatest concentrations of heavy industry in the country: shipbuilding, chemicals, engineering, glass and ceramics. Oviedo is the economic and cultural metropolis of the area, while Gijón is the main port. Cider is the local drink; salmon and trout from the mountain streams are the local delicacies.

Cantabria's chief city is Santander, which was almost destroyed by tornado and fire in 1941. The Altamira Caves, whose famous paleolithic rock paintings were the first ever found, are the wonder of this small coastal enclave.

The most easterly of the Atlantic regions of Spain and the most violently different—indeed, the most violent—is the Basque Country, which comprises the provinces of Vizcaya, Guipuzcoa and Álava and is referred to by Basque nationalists as Euskadi. This is one of the most beautiful and dangerous corners of Europe, inhabited by one of the Continent's oldest indigenous people. They speak Euskera, their own little-understood language, and shelter one of the most sophisticated terrorist organizations in the world —Euskadi Ta Askatasuna (Freedom for the Basque Homeland), known by the acronym ETA.

The land the Basques cherish is a hilly, green, damp, wooded, well-farmed region of carefully tended orchards and lush cattle pastures, with clear, fast-running streams and large homesteads called *caserías*. These are capacious houses constructed of stone, with steep roofs, long balconies, overhanging eaves to keep off the snow in winter, and room enough inside for both family and livestock.

The Basques themselves are descendants of nomads from Central Asia who first settled in the Pyrenean region 4,000 years ago. Now they show few signs of their Asiatic origins. They are taller and fairer-haired than most Spaniards. Many men wear the beret, a national symbol shared with the 100,000-plus Basques who live across the Pyrenees in France. Common, too, to both sides of the frontier are skipping dances, performed not to the Spanish guitar and castanets but to the sound of drums, trumpets and whistles.

Despite their capacity for fun, the Basques are generally a reserved and very serious people. They are also physically strong: They organize wood-chopping and stone-lifting contests for sport; and they are devotees of pelota, or jai alai, a fast and demanding ball game played in a walled court with bare hands or with wicker rackets that can hurl a small rubber ball at speeds of almost 125 miles per hour.

1

Although much of their land remains agricultural, for more than a century now the Basques have also been in the forefront of Spain's industrial development. Seven miles from the mouth of the River Nervión lies Bilbao, capital of Vizcaya province and Spain's biggest port. The discovery of iron ore in the 19th century marked the beginning of Bilbao's phenomenal growth. Iron and steel foundries and shipbuilding yards crowded along the riverbanks and up the valleys. In the boom time of the 1950s and 1960s, big multinational companies like General Electric, Firestone and Westinghouse, which were attracted by the cheap labor, invested in the area, and job opportunities became plentiful.

Since the 1960s, a worldwide slackening in demand for iron and steel products has hit the city hard. Unemployment in the mid-1980s was even higher than the national average of 22 percent. By then, the city was one of the most densely populated and heavily polluted in Europe. In their frustration, its laid-off workers and unemployed youth confronted the forces of order in clashes that became increasingly violent. Behind the hostilities in the streets, the menacing shadow of the ETA loomed large.

The roots of Basque nationalism, like those of the people themselves and the language they speak, lie deep in the

A sunny alley between blindingly white homes on the Balearic island of Iviza offers housewives a convenient spot to dry their washing. Typical of Iviza, whitewashed houses are also common throughout southern Spain: the heat of the day is reflected by the paint, helping to keep interiors cool.

mists of history, but the ETA itself was not founded until 1959. At that time, when Franco was attempting to impose centralized government from Madrid, Basque customs and traditions were either discouraged or expressly forbidden, and the Basque language could no longer be taught in schools. In a period when all political opposition to the policies of General Franco was illegal, the ETA soon found itself in the vanguard of clandestine dissent. It also quickly

turned violent. Since its inception, it has killed more than 500 people — notably, and most spectacularly, Franco's prime minister and closest collaborator, Admiral Luis Carrero Blanco, who, with his chauffeur, was blown up by a bomb planted in a tunnel under a Madrid street in 1973.

In the years since Franco's death in 1975, much has been done to placate the nationalists. Since the signing of the Statute of Guernica in 1979, the

Basques have their own Parliament, administer their own laws and raise their own taxes. The Basque flag — the red, white and green Ikurrina, which Franco outlawed — flies freely in every town, and the Basque language now has equal official status with Spanish.

But the ETA will settle for nothing less than the total independence of the Basque provinces, and so the killings have gone on. At the same time, the Spanish government has intensified its

25

antiterrorist operations, and the French Basque Country is no longer a safe refuge for fugitives on the run: In 1984, the French government agreed to hand over prisoners held in their jails on suspicion of having committed terrorist offenses in Spain. In response, the ETA stepped up its campaign of bombings and murders, both in the Basque Country itself, where it targeted principally state policemen, and in Madrid and other parts of Spain.

Yet even in their homeland, support for the strong men is waning. Most Basques now seek a political, rather than a military, solution to their problems. The moderates who dominate the main nationalist party, the PNV, are content to work for more autonomy within the framework of the Statute of Guernica. On the left, however, the ETA still has its backers in a hard core of radicals — representing perhaps 15 percent of the electorate — whose demands include the withdrawal of the national police, control of the army to be given to the Basque regional government and an amnesty for ETA members in prison. At the same time, they have taken up the objective of closer integration between the three Basque provinces and Spain's other Basque-speaking area — Navarre.

This small region, renowned for the bull stampede through the streets at the San Fermín festival in the main town of Pamplona, which Hemingway so vividly described in *The Sun Also Rises,* is sharply divided between the wet Pyrenees in the north and the dry, rain-shadow plains of the south. And the attributes of its inhabitants are similarly incompatible. Although many of its people speak Basque and observe Basque customs, the region has historically been loyal to the central authority of Castilian Spain. During Spain's murderous Civil War, the Navarrese, unlike the people of the Basque Country, fought on the Nationalist side and were rewarded by General Franco with special favors and privileges. Given such a past and such political predilections, the chances of closer liaison with the more numerous Basques some time in the future must seem slim.

Aragon, Navarre's neighbor to the east and south, was once a Mediterrean kingdom that had dominion over Sicily, Naples and parts of France; it is now confined to the three provinces of Huesca, Saragossa and Teruel. Like Navarre (and another neighbor, Catalonia), Aragon has a northern frontier formed by the high Pyrenees, including the highest peaks in the chain — among

them the 11,168-foot Pico de Aneto and the Monte Perdido, south of which lies the wild canyon of Ordeas, a National Park since 1918. Southward toward Saragossa — the metropolis of the Ebro basin, the fifth-largest city in Spain, and one of Spain's new centers of economic development — the formerly desert country has been made fertile by large-scale irrigation. Farther south, toward Teruel — a small provincial capital that suffered grievously during the Civil War — Aragon becomes part of the Iberian Cordillera, a land of tawny hillsides, ravined heights and windswept plateaus.

Between Aragon and the sea lies the region of Catalonia, occupying a triangle the size of the Netherlands in the northeast corner of Spain. It is a varied region. Below the snowy peaks and glacial lakes of the high Pyrenees, the north is green and thickly timbered. The coast above Barcelona — the Costa Brava, or "Wild Coast" — is rocky. But the shore below the city — the Costa Dorada — derives its name from the golden color of its sandy beaches. The south, which slopes down to the plains of the lower Ebro, is intensively cultivated with grain, vines, olives, fruit and garden vegetables. Yet for all of this, Catalonia is primarily an industrial re-

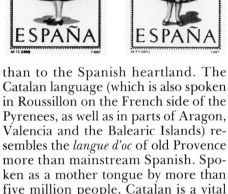

gion, the most important in Spain. It boasts a vast complex of textile, metallurgical and chemical industries and is centered on Barcelona — a city that has grown by attracting more and more workers from Andalusia and other less prosperous areas of Spain, until today roughly half its two million inhabitants are of non-Catalan stock.

Enriched by manufacturing and by tourism, Catalonia possesses a per capita income 30 percent higher than the Spanish average. The region has only 16 percent of the Spanish population, but it has been generating almost 20 percent of the nation's gross domestic product and 22 percent of industrial production: 25 percent of Spain's largest companies were based in Catalonia in 1980. In 1980, there were more students in higher education in Catalonia than anywhere else in Spain, except in Madrid. As prosperity has risen, two new waves of poor immigrant labor have occurred: unskilled, underpaid Moroccans, who have helped build the highways, followed by illegal immigrants from Africa, who do the menial jobs that the more prosperous Andalusians no longer need to do.

Cut off by mountains from the rest of Spain, Catalonia has historically been more closely tied to southern France than to the Spanish heartland. The Catalan language (which is also spoken in Roussillon on the French side of the Pyrenees, as well as in parts of Aragon, Valencia and the Balearic Islands) resembles the *langue d'oc* of old Provence more than mainstream Spanish. Spoken as a mother tongue by more than five million people, Catalan is a vital language that has always found expression in a living literature. But it is for its artists and musicians, including such 20th-century masters as painters Salvador Dalí, Joan Miró and cellist Pablo Casals, that Catalan creativity has won acknowledgment abroad.

South of Catalonia lies the area traditionally known as the Levant (the East), comprising the two regions of Valencia and Murcia. Parts of both are arid — Murcia, for example, is one of the driest areas in Europe, with less than 16 inches of rain a year. But large-scale irrigation has extended the areas under cultivation into country that was once arid steppe, transforming it into a cornucopia of oranges and lemons, almonds and grapes.

Around the city of Valencia itself, Spain's third-largest conurbation and a prosperous industrial center, irrigation projects are nothing new. There, orange trees thrive in rich soil watered by a system of channels and ducts that was built by the Romans and improved by the Arabs. Farther south lie the emerald-green paddies of the Albufera lagoon and Sueca, which grow the fat-grained rice used in the area's best-known dish, *paella Valenciana*. Even farther south, the climate is so mild that date palms, planted by the Phoenicians more than 2,000 years ago, soar in the dense palm grove of Elche. Elche is the most extensive plantation in Europe, with more than 100,000 trees, which provide not only dates but also the palm fronds that are used all over Spain for Palm Sunday processions.

The region's most lucrative resource, however, is the annual harvest of tourists. In the summer months, visitors from the north swarm over the string of resorts that line the beaches of the long-established Costa Blanca (White Coast) and the newly popular Costa del Azahar (Orange Blossom Coast). Like the other tourist coasts of Spain, the Costa Blanca has suffered greatly from the uncontrolled excesses of real estate developers — it is, the critics quip, an empire on which the cement-mixer never sets. Whole villages have been swallowed up in the mushrooming growth of hotels and apartment buildings, many of them so brash as to be a hid-

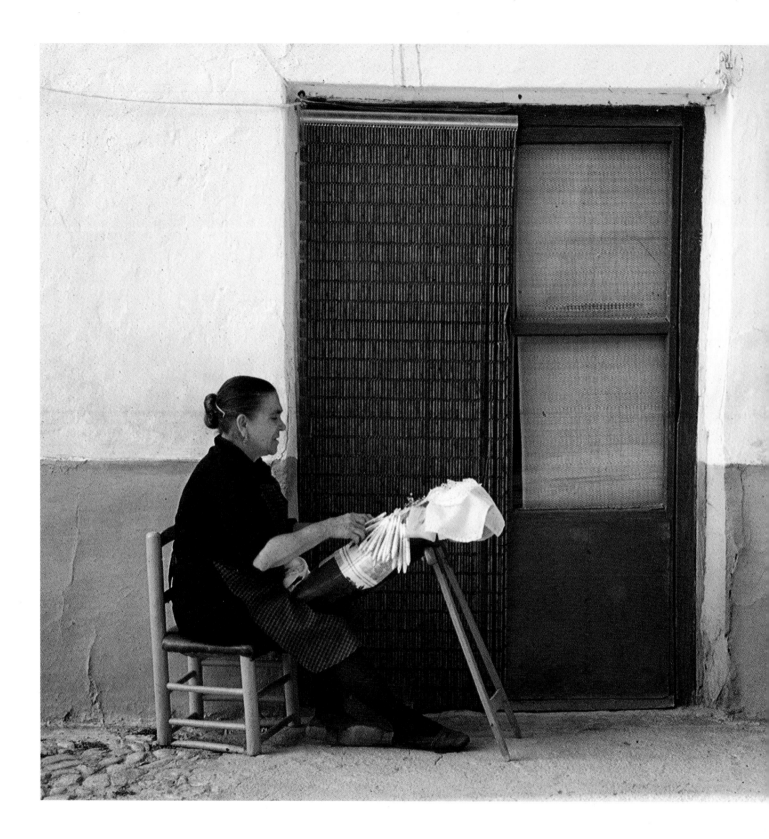

Outside her home in the village of Almagro in Castile-La Mancha, a woman dressed in the black garb of widowhood makes lace for local shops. The technique of lacemaking — whose style in this district is based on 16th-century Dutch designs — is being passed on to the young to keep the craft alive.

eous affront to their natural setting. The most popular of the Costa Blanca's resorts is Benidorm, once a small fishing village of Arabic origin and now expanding so quickly along its two huge beaches that it has almost become a city in its own right — a city based entirely on the industries of leisure and recreation. But now that Spain is no longer a low-wage country with cheap services, there are indications that, after 30 years, the Spanish tourist boom may be peaking. If so, these overdeveloped resorts may one day become ghost towns, decaying sub-Corbusier high-rise tombstones, where the sea wind rattles the rusting English pub signs and the sand dunes encroach on the abandoned boutiques and discos. This is a threat that is also looming for the Levant's neighbor, the romantic and desolate region of Andalusia.

Bounded by the forest-covered range of the Sierra Morena to the north, and the Atlantic and the Mediterreanean to the south, Andalusia covers an area of 33,675 square miles, which makes it almost as big as Portugal. But it is not a heavily populated land. Although six million people inhabit the region, the population density is only about 195 people per square mile, compared with Portugal's 281.

To most armchair travelers, Andalusia *is* Spain. It is *Carmen*, Granada's Alhambra and the Alcázar in Seville, Moorish mosques and castles, dark-eyed gypsies and whitewashed pueblos, bullfights and processions, sangria, sun and the Costa del Sol — an exotic world halfway to Africa and the East. In fact, Andalusia is all of these things and a lot more, for no other region of Spain enjoys greater variety and contrast. In the valley of the Guadalquivir, tempera-

tures of up to 113° F. (the highest in Western Europe) have been recorded. Yet only a few hours away rise the icy ramparts of the Sierra Nevada, from whose topmost peak — the 11,411-foot Mulhacén — can be glimpsed the distant Rif Mountains of Morocco. And alluvial plains so fertile that they bear three crops in a season alternate with barren limestone sierras where no rain has fallen in living memory.

The name Andalusia derives from the Arabic *Al-Andalus,* or "the land of the West," which is what it was called by the Moors who ruled the region for nearly 800 years. The Moors have been gone now for more than five centuries, but striking evidence of their occupation remains — in the genes of the people, in place names and architecture, in the cuisine and the cultivation of such foods as apricots and almonds. Like their North African neighbors across the Strait of Gibraltar, many country people still cook outside their houses on little clay braziers fueled by burning almond shells, and some of the traditional features of the houses themselves recall the Moorish past: a spacious veranda, small windows and wrought-iron grilles, a central patio — focus of family life in summer — with its blue tiles and fountain, and horseshoe arches of stucco arabesques.

The most spectacular relics of the days of the caliphs are the castles and mosques. In Granada the great 14th-century, ocher-red Arab castle of brick, stucco and rubble called the Alhambra, and the nearby white summer residence known as the Generalife, now form the only medieval Arab palace complex left in the world. In Córdoba, once the capital of Muslim Spain, the magnificent Moorish Great Mosque dominates a scene that poet Federico

García Lorca described as the most melancholy in Spain. For an atmosphere of decayed grandeur haunts this city, now merely a provincial capital but once a metropolis with over one million inhabitants at a time when London and Paris were only villages.

In Seville — 3,000 years ago a Phoenician trading center — traces remain of a capital for five succeeding civilizations (Greek, Roman, Visigoth, Moorish and Christian). Here, in the home port of Columbus and Magellan and terminus for Spain's monopoly trade in New World treasures, Moorish and Christian Renaissance monuments mix, often within the same architectural structure. The Alcázar, for example, is a fortified palace, founded by the Moors and completed by the Christians in the 14th century. Nearby is the 295-foot-tall Giralda, a 12th-century Arab minaret, topped by a lantern and a Christian statue of Faith, which was added to it during the 16th century.

Under the Moors — and the Romans before them — Andalusia was a great mining region; its mineral resources are still many and varied, including lead, coal and copper. It has also been a primary producer of fruit, grain, wine and oil; the Guadalquivir valley (from the Arabic *Wadi el Kabir*, or "the Great River") is still Spain's most extensive and fertile lowland, while the rich soils of the Campiña give the biggest yield of such dry-farming crops as wheat and sunflower seeds in the peninsula.

Paradoxically, this region has long been one of the poorer areas of Spain. A large proportion of its farming population is made up of unskilled, part-time day laborers, or *jornaleros* — landless, seasonal workers who roam the countryside searching for work and, in the past, often failed to find it. And,

THE RETURN OF THE ARABS

For almost eight centuries before their final defeat by the Christians in 1492, Moors ruled southern Spain. Now, almost 500 years later, Muslim Arabs have come back to the province of Málaga, though this time the power they wield is financial, not military.

In and around the resort of Marbella on the Costa del Sol, modern Arab businessmen and royalty from the oil-rich kingdoms of Saudi Arabia and the United Arab Emirates have been buying up land and property on a grand scale. Drawn by historical links, by good weather and by the political stability of Spain, they have made the six-mile-long strip of coast from Marbella to San Pedro de Alcántara something of a home away from home.

In the process, they have poured a fortune into the area, spending some $700 million in 1982 alone on housing and the construction of nightclubs, hotels and restaurants. Many of the private homes are palatial — none more so than the one built for King Fahd of Saudi Arabia outside Marbella, a $40-million replica of the White House, complete with helipads, a bomb shelter and a 22,000-square-foot dining room that can accommodate 500 guests.

For all their private opulence, the newcomers keep a low public profile, avoiding any involvement in local affairs. Yet signs of their presence are evident in Marbella's new mosque, for example, and in the growing number of Arabic street signs in the city's old town. For native inhabitants, though, the most appreciated gift has been the increasing prosperity that the Arabs have brought to a community already affluent from the spending of wealthy tourists.

An Arab emerges with a shopping bag from a jewelry store in Marbella. The big-spending ways of Arabs and other newcomers invigorated the market for luxury goods but also doubled real estate prices over a three-year period.

A living room designed locally for an Arab client features marble columns, Moorish plasterwork and tables with an oriental motif.

Cars await worshippers outside Marbella's new mosque, built in 1981 with money donated by a Saudi prince.

had it not been for large-scale emigration, the situation would have been far worse. In the past, the Andalusian poor, who have long had a reputation for independence and stubbornness bordering on revolt, reacted to their lot by anarchist uprisings. Later they simply left. In the 1960s, more than one million Andalusians migrated from the region in headlong flight. All across the countryside, there are whole villages that have been depopulated or completely abandoned. Houses stand derelict overlooking landscapes of miraculous beauty. Although corn cobs, pimientos and bunches of herbs still hang drying from the upstairs roof beams, and iron cooking pots and children's alphabet books lie strewn about in the rubbish, the doors swing loosely in the wind, the mice run riot, and the people have gone.

It was not lack of natural resources that impoverished Andalusia, but the kind of society that was implanted there after the Reconquest. The prevailing system of land tenure has been, and remains to this day, *latifundismo:* the division of the land into huge estates, or *latifundios,* belonging to a few wealthy, conservative families, who number less than 20,000, or scarcely 0.3 percent of the region's population. In years past, the *latifundistas* either pretended little interest in working their land or used antiquated methods and cheap labor to farm their estates, resulting in low productivity, much unemployment and poverty, and a markedly regressive society. Now when many of the *latifundistas* are turning their once-neglected estates into company farms and using modern agro-industrial techniques, the laborers are being replaced by machinery and the countryside today employs fewer people than ever.

Yet Andalusia's prospects have improved in many ways recently. It has been a chief beneficiary of the state aid distributed by the Interterritorial Compensation Fund, receiving in the mid-1980s more than a quarter of the total monies disbursed. The Socialist government at that time also introduced a program of agrarian reform designed to protect the position of the *jornalero* and to expropriate inefficiently run estates. Mass emigration has also eased the pressure of rural unemployment.

During the 1960s alone, more than one million Andalusians emigrated. They went to the industrial centers around Madrid, Barcelona and Bilbao, or abroad to France, to Britain and, above all, to Germany. Some went to Andalusia's own cities; the populations of Seville, Córdoba, Málaga, Almería, Cádiz and Huelva have all swollen over the past three decades.

Despite the region's natural riches, Andalusia's principal sources of wealth in recent decades have been from abroad — from remittances sent home by foreign workers, from the millions of tourists who have flooded into the narrow littoral of the Costa del Sol. Even much of the industrial investment in Andalusia is foreign, predominantly American. Some critics have called Andalusia a colonial world, while others, with a more optimistic outlook, have sketched golden visions of a high-technology boom time. But that is for the future. For the remaining *jornaleros,* the present is still closer in spirit to the old Andalusian melancholy of the flamenco song *Solea:*

> *Esta serraniya perra*
> *Me está jasiendo pasá*
> *Er purgatorio en la tierra.*
> (In these damned sierras
> I am fated to pass
> my purgatory on earth.)

There is another region, northwest of Andalusia, cut off from the sea by the mountains in the south and Portugal to the west, whose very name speaks of its isolation and geographical deprivation. Estremadura is popularly supposed to be derived from the Latin *terra extrema et dura* (a harsh, extreme land), a term loosely applied during the Reconquest of Spain to areas bordering the Moorish frontier.

A part of the great Meseta tableland, between the bookends of the Sierra de Gredos on the north and Sierra Morena on the south, Estremadura is not a country for the faint of heart. In the baking summer months, the flocks of sheep — the principal livestock and source of revenue in the region — are driven from their winter grazing areas into the northern hills, and the landscape takes on an eerie emptiness. The majority of the population is concentrated along the banks of the Alagón and Guadiana rivers, where the alluvial soil and intensive irrigation encourage the cultivation of tobacco, cotton, wheat

One of the delights of Spanish cuisine is *paella,* and one of the most esteemed of its many regional variations is the seafood-based Valencian version *(above).* The dish takes its name from the cast-iron pot in which it is cooked and from which it is served.

and vegetables; certain varieties of wine grapes flourish in the fertile red clay around Almendralejo.

But the pickings have never been rich in this difficult land. For much of the last 500 years, it has not even been able to feed its own sparse population, and over the centuries, many of its young men have left to seek their fortunes elsewhere. Most of the early conquistadores were sons of Estremadura: Cortés, the conqueror of Mexico; Pizarro, victor over the Inca empire of Peru and Ecuador; Núñez de Balboa, discoverer of the Pacific; Orellana, navigator of the Amazon.

If Estremadura is on the periphery of Spain, the very heart and hub of the peninsula is the high, umber-colored Meseta country to the south of the Central Cordillera. Here, there are five provinces redolent of the Spanish past and the Spanish soul: Cuenca, Ciudad-Real, Guadalajara, Toledo and Albacete. Traditionally known collectively as New Castile, they are now grouped into the Autonomous Community of Castile-La Mancha. In this region, the sense of Africa is strong; not even the Serengeti Plains can boast a wider horizon or conjure a greater sense of infinite space. The climate is continental, which is to say it is dry and scorching in summer, when every road bears a mirage, and freezing in winter, when searing winds and driving snow sweep from one end of the plateau to the other.

Castile-La Mancha is country they call *secano* — unirrigated. But it is not barren. Fields of grain stretch as far as the eye can see. Vines — from whose grapes vast quantities of Valdepeñas wine are fermented — and acre upon acre of purple-flowering saffron cover the plains of La Mancha (from the Arabic *manxa,* meaning "parched earth"). Olive trees stand in perfect, straight lines like regiments of gnarled and arthritically bent old troopers. Don Quixote was a knight of La Mancha, a quintessential Spanish hero from the Spanish heartland: Windmills like the ones he attempted to lance still

1

stand flailing on the horizon, grinding the grain. And in the middle of this limitless tableland lies the country's first city, Madrid.

Madrid is in the dead center of Spain, surrounded by a virtual desert. At an altitude of 2,130 feet, it is the highest capital city in Europe. Even after it had been declared the capital of Spain by royal decree in the 16th century, Madrid grew slowly and it would be almost three centuries before the city developed into the true heart of the country and a metropolis of international importance. Today, Madrid is a modern, sprawling conurbation of more than four million people, the financial and administrative center of Spain and the heart of its communications system.

In recent years, Madrid has experienced something of a population explosion; the number of its inhabitants has more than doubled since 1960. Such sudden growth has left its mark in spreading suburbs, congested traffic, increased pollution and an apparently endless proliferation of construction sites. It has also speeded up the pace of the city. New banks, large department stores and foreign restaurants have brought a fresh flurry of activity to the city's center.

Yet Madrid continues to move to a different rhythm than that of other capitals. However hectic its days may be, the city still takes time out for a leisurely lunch. In addition, its citizens tend to go to bed later than their counterparts elsewhere. Restaurants are at their busiest after 10 in the evening; movie theaters are filled to capacity for the 10:30 p.m. showing. Café life continues to flourish, both at midday and between seven and nine o'clock in the evening, when Madrileños like to enjoy an apértif before sitting down to din-

ner. And the crowded bars, known as *tascas*, are full of boisterous drinkers into the wee hours.

The city has its share of monuments, among them one of the world's great art galleries, the Prado. It also boasts a wonderful 17th-century square, the Plaza Mayor, once a venue for bullfights and the burning of heretics, now a café-lined pedestrian precinct. But ultimately it is the bustling street life that stays in the mind — the crowds jostling in the alleyways of the Rastro flea market, filling the shops, restaurants and theaters of the Gran Vía, strolling in the evenings along the shaded promenades of the Retiro park.

North of Madrid, the vast plateau of the Meseta stretches out through the provinces of Old Castile, now known administratively as Castile-Leon. Old Castile is, for the most part, a region of endless horizons and widely scattered villages, with great plains of wheat and rye in the north and farms of sheep and fighting bulls in the south. In the adjoining region of La Rioja (a contraction of Rio Oja) lies the fertile Ebro River valley, whose vineyards produce Spain's finest and best-known red wine, as well as 95 percent of the country's asparagus exports. But it is the cities that are the great sights of this central part of Spain: Avila, Spain's highest and coldest provincial capital and the birthplace of one of the Roman Catholic Church's greatest mystics, Saint Theresa; the ancient Gothic city of Burgos, where the warrior hero El Cid is buried; Salamanca, a marvelous university city of spires and domes, ancient squares and elaborate façades, conquered in turn by Hannibal, Napoleon and Wellington; Segovia, with the finest working Roman aqueduct in the world. In these and other beautiful old

cities, the proud, reserved Castilian physiognomy, familiar from portraits by Velázquez and El Greco, can still be seen in the streets today.

Beyond the mainland frontiers of Spain, the old Spanish imperium has shrunk to almost nothing since the days when Madrid ruled the New World from California to Chile. The farthest flung of Spain's few remaining overseas territories are the Canary Islands, a volcanic archipelago just to the north of the Tropic of Cancer and only 62 miles from the Atlantic coast of southern Morocco. Although they are 10 times nearer to the continent of Africa than to the mother country, the Canaries have been administered as an integral part of metropolitan Spain since they were first claimed by the Spanish in the early 15th century.

The largest islands in the Canaries are Grand Canary, Fuerteventura and Lanzarote in the east, and Tenerife, La Palma, Gomera and Hierro in the west. All are hot the year round and several are high and ruggedly mountainous; the seasonally snow-capped and periodically active volcano of Pico de Teide on Tenerife is, at 12,200 feet, Spain's highest peak. Though inhabited by Europeans, the islands retain an African character, with rain-starved cactus deserts on their south sides and, on the north, a lush, tropical plant cover enriched by volcanic ash. World-famous for their bananas and tomatoes, the islands have long been a favorite destination for tourists from Europe, who are today their principal industry.

Much nearer to the mainland are the Balearic Islands of Majorca, Minorca and Iviza. Majorca and Iviza are hilly and wooded; Minorca, geologically a part of Sardinia, is lower, flatter and

On a Sunday morning outside the Gothic cathedral of Barcelona, scores of people join hands to perform the traditional Catalan dance known as the *sardana*. Based on a pattern of long and short steps, the dancers' measures are performed to the sound of wind instruments and small drums.

more heathlike. As far as character and climate are concerned, the locals put it another way: "Majorca looks to Spain, Minorca looks to France, Iviza looks to Africa." All are agricultural, and all enjoy hot summers and some of the cleanest, clearest waters in the Mediterranean. They are now major tourist attractions, especially Majorca, one of the first places to experience large-scale tourism in Europe, whose coastline has undergone an inevitable metamorphosis as a result (though the lovely interior remains surprisingly unspoiled).

Two tiny Spanish enclaves are set in the African landscape. Melilla and Ceuta are both Spanish army bases and all that is left of Spain's colonial presence in Morocco. Conversely, two foreign territories abut on the Spanish mainland. One is the minute principality of Andorra in the heart of the Pyrenees. A little larger than the Isle of Wight, with a population of slightly more than 30,000 Catalan-speaking farmers and stock-raisers, it has been jealously independent of both Spain and France since the Middle Ages and seems likely to remain so forever.

A more awkward situation is that of Gibraltar, a limestone peninsula commanding the narrow entrance to the Mediterranean, which was one of the two Pillars of Hercules that, in ancient times, marked the western limits of the known world. Only three miles long and about half a mile wide, Gibraltar was captured by the Royal Navy in 1704 and ceded to the British in 1713, but the Spanish have laid claim to it on both geographical and historical grounds ever since. In 1969, the Spanish side of the border was closed on Franco's orders and not reopened until 1985. For their part, the British felt unable to hand Gibraltar back, since the great

1

majority of the Gibraltarians have expressed a desire to remain under British rule whether the Spaniards — or for that matter, the British — like it or not.

Given the diversity of the land of Spain, it may seem perverse to seek common characteristics in the Spanish people. Yet some personality traits, more cultural than genetic, can be traced through the nation's history and its differing regions. On the positive side, there is the elaborate courtesy and cool, aloof dignity traditionally cultivated by the *caballero,* or country gentleman — virtues derived from medieval chivalry, whose influence lingered on here centuries after it had been abandoned by the rest of Europe. There is, too, the long-suffering patience and stoical endurance of the peasantry, eking a living from the unrewarding soil. In a darker vein, melancholy and nostalgic longing, called *soledad,* run like a leitmotif through much of Spanish life, and a streak of violence and cruelty is also evident. This is not a land of compromise; instead, the choice is *todo o nada,* all or nothing, black or white.

Much of the Spanish personality is the direct consequence of the deprivation it has endured through centuries of neglect, civil strife, dictatorship and isolation from the rest of Europe. Other characteristics can be seen as the product of the poverty brought about by the harsh geography and lack of resources, of hunger, insecurity and hopelessness under the domination of a ruling class that still held to the strict ideals of a militant Catholicism.

All this is changing, though, because Spain is currently in the midst of a transformation as profound as any that has affected the country in the past four centuries. The catalyst was the death of General Franco, who throughout his long rule had resolutely set his gaze on the glorious past, the haughty Catholic Spain of the nation's golden age in the 16th century. Under his authoritarian rule, the land was isolated, conservative and inward-looking.

But since his death, an extraordinary metamorphosis has taken place. One of the world's most enduring dictatorships has been replaced without violence by a progressive democracy with a king, Juan Carlos I, as constitutional head of state and guarantor of the people's sovereignty. Political parties and labor unions have been legalized, and within two years of Juan Carlos' accession in 1975, the Spanish people went to the polls for the first general election in 40 years. In December 1978, a new democratic constitution was promulgated. Since then, the parliamentary system has gradually become more secure; in the general election of October 1982, Spanish voters peacefully elected their first left-wing government since 1936 in a landslide victory for PSOE (Spanish Socialist Workers' party).

The new Spain that has emerged with the ending of the Franco dictatorship sometimes seems a different land from the one the general ruled. The country is still split politically between the right and left, but less murderously so than it has been in the past. The growth of a middle class has helped close the gap between rulers and proletariat that was once a cause of violent confrontation. Spain is now a bourgeois, capitalist social democracy, and a more stable society than it has been for many centuries past.

It is at the personal level that the somersault of Spanish society seems most striking. Thirty years ago, a woman wearing a bikini might be hauled into the nearest police station on a charge of public immorality; today, women lie naked on nudist beaches. If the women of today have more freedom, it is for the young that things have changed radically — pot, hard drugs, hard rock, soft porn, blue jeans — life is not what it was. The contemporary Western way of life is replacing the traditional Spanish one. Even the siesta is disappearing. The three-hour-long lunch break and post-prandial nap in the heat of the day are becoming a thing of the past, as the government calls for a continuous eight-hour work day and city workers find the interval away from the office cut short by the time it takes to travel between their jobs and their homes in the suburbs.

Among the changes in the new Spain that promise to have the most unforeseeable but profound consequences is a much closer integration with Western Europe after 400 years of often self-imposed isolation. Spain became a member of the North Atlantic Treaty Organization (NATO) in 1982, although not a wholly committed one. In June 1985, accords were signed to admit Spain (along with Portugal) to the European Economic Community.

What the long-term effects of this new orientation will be remain to be seen. At the time, however, the Spanish press greeted the event with guarded affirmations of nationalism. One cartoon showed Spain standing on the Pyrenees dressed as a matador waving a cape at the rest of Europe. Another depicted the EEC countries as a row of placid cows in a milking stall — except for one, which was unmistakably a Spanish fighting bull. The message of such gentle gibes was clear: Spain was still different, even if she was now part of the European community. □

A dove wings its way past a statue of an angel in Maria Luisa Park in Seville. Named after a duchess who donated half of her palace gardens to the city in 1893, the park — with its tree-lined walks, pools and fountains — offers welcome relief from the summer heat.

Almond orchards bloom on the foothills of Spain's highest mountain range, the Sierra Nevada. Almond and apricot trees were first brought to Andalusia by the Moors, who ruled Spain from 711 to 1492.

PERSPECTIVES OF A HIGH, DRY COUNTRY

From its towering northern peaks to its sun-washed southern shores, Spain's richly varied landscape unfolds across the Iberian Peninsula. The steep-shouldered Pyrenees, stretching along the French border, define a natural frontier with the Continent. The coastlines that fall away from the Pyrenees' foothills provide a rocky Atlantic exposure and sandy Mediterranean beaches — almost 1,900 miles of shoreline in all. Inland, the parched expanses of the Meseta plain, a lofty plateau with an average altitude of about 2,000 feet, dominate the Spanish heartland.

In the interior of the vast Meseta, windmills punctuate a bleak horizon of tableland, but on its perimeters, farm country gradually replaces arid steppe. The Ebro River slices across northern Spain, creating a fertile valley and watering the vineyards of La Rioja. This wine country borders on the Basque region, agricultural uplands reaching to the Bay of Biscay between the Pyrenees and the Cantabrian mountains. Here, as in neighboring Galicia, the temperate maritime climate nurtures lush, undulating fields and forests. To the south of the Meseta, the Andalusian hills rise to the Sierra Nevada. The range includes the Spanish mainland's highest peak, the Cerro de Mulhacén, which looks south across the Mediterranean beaches of the Costa del Sol to the Strait of Gibraltar.

Offshore, in the Mediterranean Sea, lies the Balearic archipelago — Majorca, Minorca, Iviza, Formentera and more than 100 rocky islets. The islands, deeply carved with cliffs and coves, are actually an eastern extension of the Andalusian mountains, cut off from the mainland millennia ago. Spain also has a foothold in the Atlantic Ocean, where the 13 Canary Islands lie about 680 miles southwest of Cádiz. The topography of these volcanic islands varies widely, from bare, wind-sculpted rock to luxuriant tropical vegetation.

On the dry plains of Castile-La Mancha, a road winds between fields reclaimed for agriculture by irrigation.

Windmills line an exposed ridge in the La Mancha district. First introduced from Holland in the 1570s, the mills were used to grind grain; many are now falling into disrepair.

Raised on stone stilts to protect its contents from rats and dampness, a Galician *hórreo*, or grain store, is adorned with twin crosses rivaling those of a neighboring church. Such long, narrow granaries are a feature of the region, which is rich in corn and grain.

High in the Picos de Europa range of northern Spain, the hamlet of Las Vegas de Sotres straggles down a stony track. Its granite huts are occupied only during the summer months, by families whose cattle graze in the nearby mountain pastures.

Less than 15 miles from the French border in the foothills of the Pyrenees, the town of Viella lies on one of the minor mountain passes connecting the two countries. Until 60 years ago, the community, in the northernmost corner of Catalonia, was connected to the outside world only by bridle paths.

In the northeast, ridges of the high Pyrenees sweep down to enclose deep, narrow valleys. The mountains, which separate Spain and France, have contributed to the Iberian Peninsula's isolation from the rest of Europe.

44

In the Basque Country, a *caserío* — a group of traditional wide-gabled dwellings built to hold both farm families and their livestock — spreads over the wooded slopes of the Cantabrian hills. The farmhouses are hemmed in by densely cultivated fields of corn and lush grazing meadows for cattle.

46

In the wine-producing region of La Rioja, a tiny northern district, vineyards surround a village. The area produces the nation's most highly regarded vintages, most of them light, red wines lengthily matured in oak.

47

Snow-clad even in midsummer, the
Pico de Teide, a dormant volcano,
soars 12,200 feet high on Tenerife in
the Canary Islands, about 220 miles
west of the Moroccan coast. In the fore-
ground, an eroded cone of volcanic
rock balances precariously above two
dwarfed passers-by.

48

The lighthouse at Cap Formentor, the northernmost point of Majorca, flashes a warning light toward the mainland 125 miles away. Majorca is the largest of the Balearic Islands, which have been an integral part of Spain since the 14th century and are now a mecca for Mediterranean-bound tourists.

A 16th-century relief in Granada's Alhambra Palace celebrates the triumphant entry of Ferdinand of Aragon and his consort, Isabella of Castile, into the last Moorish stronghold in Spain. The taking of the city in 1492 ended the Reconquista — the gradual Christian reconquest of Muslim lands.

THE BLOODSTAINED PAST

With the coming of the Phoenicians in about the ninth century B.C., Spain first entered recorded history. The Iberian Peninsula had been inhabited long before that time. There are traces of Neanderthals dating from before the last Ice Age, and the Paleolithic hunters who succeeded them were the start of an unbroken human line that led to the blend of Celts and Iberians who populated Spain in early historic times. But evidence of these early people is fragmentary: Records include a few glorious cave paintings, notably at Altamira on the north coast, and some metal artifacts, the product of extensive copper and bronze workings.

Most probably, it was Spanish metal that attracted the Phoenicians, who built the trading city of Gadir on the site of modern Cádiz. Later, the Greeks established colonies, mostly on the coast of Catalonia. Neither the Phoenicians nor the Greeks, however, seriously attempted to dominate the peninsula and its people. The next arrivals had more imperial ambitions.

Carthage, a North African city-state, had itself once been a Phoenician colony, but by the sixth century B.C., it was an independent and expanding mercantile empire. Beginning with the existing Phoenician settlements, the Carthaginians soon incorporated most of coastal Spain into their dominions. But, like their predecessors, the Carthaginians had little to do with the fiercely primitive tribes of the interior.

Before long, they had more to contend with than hostile tribesmen, for by the third century B.C., the Romans had begun their own imperial expansion. And the Mediterranean world was apparently not big enough for both empires. It was from Spain that the Carthaginian general Hannibal launched his legendary attack, complete with war elephants, across the Alps, and it was Spanish troops who provided the bulk of his army. But Hannibal's brilliant campaign in Italy brought no long-term success. In 214 B.C., the Romans retaliated by invading Spain; by 206 B.C., the last Carthaginian city — Cádiz — had surrendered, and the long era of Roman Spain had begun.

The Romans discovered in their turn, however, that it was one thing to take Spain from the Carthaginians, but another to take it from the Spaniards. Although areas along the Mediterranean coast were rapidly assimilated into Rome's empire, it was almost two centuries before the hinterland was under control, and even then, the Basque Country remained almost untouched. In most regions, the Roman armies met ferocious resistance from tribesmen — and women — who often chose death over surrender. "They prefer war to ease," remarked one Roman historian, "and should they lack foes without, seek them within."

Nevertheless, Roman rule eventually brought Spain a long period of peace and a unity it had never known before and has seldom known since. Hispania, as the Romans called it, was the wealthiest province of the empire and had one of the richest cultures. It was the birthplace of some of the greatest Latin writers, among them the epigrammatist Martial, the tragedian Seneca and the poet Lucan, as well as three emperors. And in later times, Hispania provided popes, because Christianity, perhaps taught by the Apostle Paul himself, reached the province early and, after overcoming the usual initial persecution, grew deep and lasting roots.

By the end of the fourth century A.D., however, a combination of internal decadence and pressure from the barbarian peoples beyond its frontiers threatened the existence of the empire. Spanish-born Emperor Theodosius was its last effective defender. After his death in 395, a patchwork of tribes — Alani from the Russian steppe, Vandals and Suevi from Germany — swarmed into the western section of his domain. By 409, they had reached Spain.

Paradoxically, Hispania was saved from complete disintegration by another Germanic tribe: the Visigoths. Ostensibly in the empire's service, they drove out their rivals, and once they were securely in possession, renounced even token allegiance to the enfeebled imperial authority. This new Visigothic kingdom was a ramshackle affair, imposed by a few hundred thousand "free warriors" and their families on a settled, orderly population of perhaps nine million. Remarkably, it endured almost three centuries.

Kingship in Visigothic Spain was, in theory, elective, and the factional conflicts generated every time there was a vacancy on the throne in the capital of Toledo finally led to the Visigoths' downfall. In 711, one thwarted faction sought help from outside Spain —

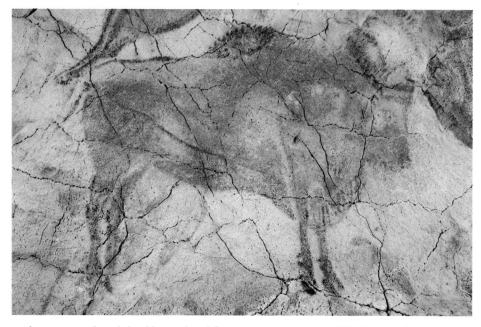

productivity reached new levels. Moorish rulers erected a number of splendid cities, the greatest of which was their capital, Córdoba.

The one thing the Moors did not bring, even to their own domains, was political unity. Their rule in Spain was riven by factionalism and revolt. Only briefly, in the 10th century, was an undivided hegemony imposed over all of Al-Andalus, as Arab Spain was known. Even then, the mighty caliphs of Córdoba could not eradicate entirely the Christian realms to the north. Indeed, the financial strains of the enormous military effort they undertook in order to achieve total victory were partly responsible for the disintegration of the Caliphate early in the 11th century.

Al-Andalus was never again united as a single power, and the Christians were able, at last, to play an increasingly important role: The age of the Reconquista (Reconquest) was well under way. But the retaking of Islamic Spain was never the coherent movement some history books suggest. The kings and counts of the north spent at least as much time fighting one another as they did attacking the Muslims, and the shifting pattern of alliances and betrayals often crossed religious lines.

Perhaps the best example of the bloodthirsty complexity of Reconquista politics is the real-life career of El Cid, the semilegendary Christian hero who was the subject of the 12th-century poem that became Spain's national epic. El Cid — the title itself is Arabic, from *sayyid*, meaning "lord" — was Rodrigo Díaz de Bivar, a warrior vassal of King Alfonso VI of Castile and Leon. He won his early fame fighting for Alfonso against the Muslims, but eventually, he quarreled bitterly with his overlord and transferred his allegiance to

and got more than it had bargained for.

By that year, the Arab enthusiasts of the new faith of Islam had reached North Africa in strength, and it was to them that the kingmakers turned. The Arabs, led by Tarik ibn Zeyad, seized the opportunity and launched a force of 7,000 men across the narrow strait at the mouth of the Mediterranean into Spain. The Arabs landed near a rock that they named Jabal Tarik (Mount Tarik) after their leader, a name later corrupted to Gibraltar. In only five years, Tarik's men, reinforced by adventurous coreligionists from as far away as Yemen and Persia, had driven Spain's former rulers out of the south and into a tiny enclave in the northern territory of Asturias, establishing an Arab emirate over most of the country.

For a time, it seemed that the Muslim tide would sweep beyond Spain and engulf all Europe. But the Frankish victory at Poitiers in 732 forced the invaders back into Spain, and vigorous counterattacks by the unconquered Christians of Asturias soon recovered most of Leon. During the next two centuries, the Douro River marked the uneasy frontier between the two hostile cultures; meanwhile, the Christians who remained in Moorish Spain learned to live with their new rulers. Generally, it was not too difficult. Christians who clung to their old faith were seldom seriously persecuted, and many — in the far south, the majority — chose to convert to the faith of their masters.

Indeed, for many Spaniards, Moorish rule was an improvement. The Arabs brought with them habits of civilized living that had more in common with the Roman Empire in its heyday than with the rustic, tribal ways of the Visigoths. Moorish landowners repaired irrigation systems neglected since Roman times, and agricultural

the Muslim king of Saragossa. Toward the end of his life, he struck out as an independent warlord, seizing Valencia from the Moors and holding it in his own right until his death.

At any one time in the 11th and 12th centuries, the Iberian Peninsula would have seemed an inchoate swirl of civil war: Christian against Christian and Muslim against Muslim, as well as Christian against Muslim. Nevertheless, the progress of the Reconquista was inexorable. By 1248, when Seville fell to Ferdinand of Castile, Al-Andalus had been reduced to the little southwestern kingdom of Granada. The rest of the peninsula was shared by four Christian states: Portugal, Castile, Ara-gon and Navarre. Primarily because of this division, it was almost 250 years before the remnants of Muslim rule were finally overwhelmed.

In spite of the turbulence, the era was extraordinarily rich in cultural achievement. On the Islamic side, Córdoba made up in intellectual grandeur what it had lost in military power: Arabic and Hebrew scholars and philosophers — the two best remembered are Averroes and Maimonides — were beginning to unlock the secrets of the lost learning of classical Greece. In Christian Spain, Toledo had developed a great school of translators and a center of philosophical studies. Thus, the work of Aristotle, for example, was rendered into Arabic by Muslims and from Arabic into Latin by Christians. Between them, the two hostile civilizations relighted a torch of learning that was to take Europe out of the Dark Ages.

In Muslim and in Christian Spain alike, Jewish communities settled in the land for centuries past had made contributions to the arts and learning out of all proportion to their numbers. But after the Christian victories of the 1200s, the tolerance previously accorded Judaism began to ebb. By 1391, there were massacres in all the Christian kingdoms, and most of the surviving Jews were forcibly converted — an act of religious cruelty that was to have lasting consequences.

2

It was, in a sense, an attempt to impose some sort of cultural homogeneity in a land where, within as well as between the kingdoms, political divisions ran deep. As a result of centuries of warfare, not only towns but even most villages were strongly fortified, and there were jealously guarded traditions of local independence throughout Spain. Royal authority was nowhere absolute. Even in Castile, the most centralized of the kingdoms, powerful noblemen regularly used civil war to defend their privileges.

However, there was increasing recognition of the need for unified government. In 1469, when Isabella, heir to the throne of Castile, married Ferdinand, King of Aragon, the match was generally welcomed. But predictably, the queen's accession was disputed. Five years of civil war ensued before, in 1479, the two monarchs were able to extend the benefits of joint rule to their realms. It was a long way from political union, but it was a start. It marked the beginning of modern Spain.

The first task Ferdinand and Isabella set themselves was the completion of the Reconquest. Little by little, Muslim Granada's territory crumbled before the combined advance of Aragon and Castile, and the city of Granada fell in 1492, after an 18-month siege. Its last Islamic ruler, Abu-Abdullah, "fled disguised as a woman from the city he lacked the manhood to defend," his Arab enemies alleged; the spot from which he caught his final glimpse of Granada is still known as "The Last Sigh of the Moor." In recognition of their services to Christendom, the pope bestowed on Ferdinand and Isabella the title, the Catholic Monarchs.

While their armies were clearing the Moors from Spain, the Catholic Monarchs lived up to their name by making a rigorous drive for ideological purity. The campaign they launched was to endure for more than 350 years, and it earned a reputation for such implacable ferocity that it inspires shudders to this day. Its instrument was the Holy Office of the Inquisition.

In theory an agency of the Church devoted to the suppression of heresy, the Spanish Inquisition was in fact largely under the monarchy's control. Set up in 1478 at Isabella's request, its immediate task was to deal with the *conversos* — descendants of Spanish Jews converted a century before, many of whom paid no more than lip service to their enforced Catholicism. (A simpler approach was adopted in dealing with those Jews who refused even nominally to accept baptism; they were expelled en masse, a move that cost the nation about 170,000 of its most economically active citizens.)

The agency's brief was soon extended to include Christian heretics. Thousands of victims passed through its grim process — from denunciation to secret arrest to interrogation under torture — emerging, perhaps many years later, to the horror of an *auto de fe,* literally an "act of faith." The act developed into an elaborate ritual that usually started with a procession to the main plaza of the city where the Inquisition was in session. Masses would be celebrated and sermons would be read. Then, after ceremonial oaths of obedience to the Holy Office, the prisoners would be sentenced. The most common punishments meted out were confiscation of property and imprisonment, but in severe cases, the judgment could be much harsher. Between 1487 and 1498 — when the infamous Tomás de Torquemada, the first Grand Inquisitor, was in office — about 2,000 men and women were burned to death.

The atmosphere of suspicion and fear was pervasive, and nobody in Spain felt safe from the Inquisition's informers and agents. Even Ignatius of Loyola — who founded the Jesuits and who was canonized a century later — was arrested twice on suspicion of heresy. At one stage during Torquemada's reign of terror, Pope Sixtus IV felt bound to intervene, but his pleas for moderation fell on deaf ears: The Catholic Monarchs had a weapon too valuable to abandon, a useful arm of royal power and a force for unity in a nation that needed all the cohesion it could get. And, over the next century, the period of its greatest power, the Inquisition became a pervasive system of thought control that paralyzed intellectual development and left Spain outside the mainstream of European ideas.

But that was for the future. At the end of the 15th century, Spain was still destined for greatness, not paralysis. The capture of Granada in 1492 was cause enough for triumph, but in that same year, one of Isabella's minor projects also bore fruit. Almost casually, she had financed the voyage of an apparently demented Genoese navigator called Christopher Columbus, who had sworn to find a passage to the Far East by sailing westward across the open and unknown Atlantic. The voyage turned out to be the most successful speculation in history. For the relatively trifling sum invested in the expedition, the Catholic Monarchs found themselves the rulers of a whole new world.

Neither Isabella nor Ferdinand lived long enough to realize just how much wealth was to be won in the Americas, and they devoted their later years to

Setting out in 1229 to reclaim Majorca from the Moors, King James I of Aragon confers with his knights. His successful expedition was recorded 50 years later in a fresco in the Palacio Berenguer de Aguilar in Barcelona.

empire building nearer home. Aragon had had an interest in Sicily and southern Italy since the 13th century. Now Ferdinand annexed the kingdom of Naples. In 1512, when he took over Navarre on the Iberian Peninsula itself, he extended Spain to its modern boundaries and made it the most powerful force in the western Mediterranean.

The death of Ferdinand in 1516 brought Spain even more imperial responsibility than had his life. He was succeeded by his grandson Charles, who was also heir to the Austrian Hapsburg dynasty and, from 1519, as Charles V, the Holy Roman Emperor. Charles had inherited an extraordinary

patchwork of territory all over Europe, including Austria, the Netherlands and much of Burgundy, as well as Spain, Naples, Milan, Sardinia and Sicily. Although he was only a teenager at his accession, Charles had a strong sense of imperial destiny: He was determined to hold onto every square inch of his domains and to extend them wherever possible. To achieve this goal, he needed money and soldiers — and a lot of them, since his strategic position in the European web of dynastic alliances and antagonisms ensured his involvement in every quarrel on the Continent. Spain was to provide both.

The immediate result of Charles's

succession was an outbreak of popular revolts in several Castilian towns that objected to the financial demands of the king's chancellor. These towns formed a league and set up a revolutionary government that demanded the right to discuss all matters relating to the welfare of the state. The Spanish nobility, affronted by the imposition of a foreign king and his court, did little to check this so-called *comunero* revolt — until more radical elements tried to foment similar unrest on the nobles' estates. Only in 1521, a year after the Castilian revolt started, did the aristocracy raise an army and put an end to what historians now describe as "the

FORTRESSES ACROSS THE LANDSCAPE

Spain is dotted with castles that bear witness to the conflicts of its past. Some have been restored, but many lie open to the sky or crumble on forgotten hillsides.

During the wars of the Reconquest, thousands of strongholds were built to secure conquests and defend against counterattack. But once the Arab threat had been contained, the castles of the 13th and 14th centuries became primarily fortified bases for noble families embroiled in the conflicts of neighboring Christian rulers. Plain square towers and rambling enceinte walls *(top row, far left, and bottom row, right)* are typical of these fortresses designed more for strength than for comfort.

The 15th century was the great age of the castle-palaces of the nobility. Defensive strength was still paramount: Massive walls with round towers *(top row, right)* and loopholes for muskets *(bottom row, center)* helped to protect against the new threat of artillery. But at the same time a new interest in the beauty of the building led to more symmetrical designs, with decorative detail that often showed Moorish influence *(top row, center)*. Finally, when a strong central power emerged in the 16th century, the sway of local potentates declined, and the long chapter of castle building in Spain was over.

Most of Spain's great fortresses are located in Castile, the historical heart of the country. Shown here, from left to right are: *(top row)* the castle of Magana in Soria; Manzanares el Real near Madrid; the keep and rampart of Belmonte in Cuenca; *(middle row)* the carefully restored Torija castle northeast of Madrid; the Moorish Alcazaba at Guadix in Andalusia; the Alcázar of Segovia; *(bottom row)* the castle of Knights Templar at Ponferrada; the Castillo de la Mota at Medina del Campo in Valladolid; Molina de Aragon in Guadalajara.

first true revolution of modern times."

Charles's imperial ambitions were to remain a heavy burden for a country with little natural wealth. But just as Charles was coming into his inheritance, Spanish soldier-explorers in the New World were finding what seemed an inexhaustible supply of prosperity. For a generation after Columbus' expedition, Spanish settlement and exploitation had been confined to the West Indies and Panama. But in 1519, Hernán Cortés discovered the ancient and highly civilized Aztec empire in Mexico. By 1521, he and his band of a few hundred adventurers had conquered it, a feat that surprised the Spaniards as much as it did the Aztecs. A dozen years later, Francisco Pizarro and even fewer men annihilated the equally ancient Inca civilization of Peru.

Cortés and Pizarro were the archetypal conquistadors — ruthless soldiers of fortune of modest social rank, hardened in Spain's endless wars, determined to seek glory and gold in the unknown Americas. In the name of God, Spain and their own quick-tempered honor, they carved out an unprecedented, worldwide empire that, by the mid-16th century, included most of Central America between present-day Mexico and Peru.

For the original inhabitants, of course, the conquistadors were an unmitigated disaster. Massacred by the invaders and attacked by European diseases to which they had no resistance, their societies collapsed in chaos. The majority of those who survived were reduced to virtual slavery in the fields or in the colossal silver mines of Mexico and Peru: a bedrock of human misery underlying the greatness of 16th-century Spain.

The image of Spain in its period of

In this 15th-century painting, Jews who have refused to renounce their faith are burned at the stake; two others are led away in the conical hats of the converted. When it began its activities in 1481, the Inquisition's primary task was to investigate the sincerity of Jewish converts to Christianity.

world dominion is an unattractive compound of the brutal conquistador armed with whip and sword and the grim Inquisitor with his torture chamber and stake. There were also contemporary Spaniards like Bartolomé de las Casas, a colonist turned priest who devoted his life to seeking justice for the oppressed in the New World, and who refused to allow Spain's crimes to be hidden. As for the Inquisition, it was at least impartial in its punishment of heretics of whatever rank and was more popular among ordinary Spaniards than the rural courts of law.

However, such arguments were for later times. For Charles and his campaigns, the wealth of the Indies was a gift from providence that soon became essential. To the ceaseless wars he waged to control his inheritance was added the burden of his greatest title. As Holy Roman Emperor, he was the ostensible leader of secular Christendom. His reign coincided with the beginnings of the Protestant Reformation, and in a vain attempt to preserve the spiritual unity of Europe, he was repeatedly plunged into struggles, both religious and fratricidal. All the treasure of the Aztec and Inca civilization was not enough for Charles's war chest. "I cannot be sustained except by my kingdoms in Spain," he declared in 1540. It fell to Castile, his Spanish power base, to provide most of the sustenance he required, and in time, the drain on Castilian resources helped to cripple the kingdom economically.

The traditions of the Spanish nobility, the *hidalgos* — from *hijos de algo*, meaning the "sons of somebody" — did not help the country's economic plight. They invested in land without developing agriculture, preferring careers in the army, Church and civil service to "vulgar" commerce. Charles bought their loyalty with the rewards of office.

Many found a career in Europe's most efficient army. In the 1530s, Spain's military forces were regrouped into the dreaded *tercios* — self-sufficient mixed units of some 3,000 pikemen, swordsmen and musketeers, trained to fight in close, well-drilled formation. The *tercios* outclassed every opponent: On the battlefield, as often as not, they literally walked over their enemies.

But there were too many battlefields. Charles fought in France, in Germany, in Italy and North Africa. He fought the Turks; he fought the Protestants; at one point, this Catholic Monarch and Holy Roman Emperor fought even the Pope. By 1555, weary and dispirited about his hopes of a united Europe, he gave up his crown and retired to the remote monastery of San Jerónimo de Yuste, more than 100 miles west of Madrid. Before abdicating, he divided up his vast realm. The German land, and the title of Emperor, went to his brother Ferdinand, while Spain and its dependencies — the Franche-Comté, the Low Countries, Milan, Naples and Sicily — were bequeathed to his son Philip.

In the reign of Philip II, the nation reached its imperial zenith — and heard the first rumblings of future disaster. By the mid-century, the new king's Spanish empire was becoming as expensive to maintain as his father's more heterogeneous dominions. On land, his *tercios* were as invincible as ever; but at sea other, lesser powers — notably England — were beginning to challenge Spain's hegemony. Beginning in 1564, it was necessary to assign strong escorts to the treasure convoys crossing the Atlantic, and even when the bullion arrived safely, it was never enough to satisfy the exchequer. Easy money from the Indies had lured men's minds away from the kind of steady but unspectacular economic development the country desperately needed, and had created a raging inflation. In 1557, the state announced a moratorium on its debts, and new and stifling taxes.

The imposition of these taxes on Spain's Netherlands territories was one of a number of reasons for a grumbling rebellion there. In 1568, Philip sent his commander, the Duke of Alba, at the head of an army of his best Spanish and Italian troops, to root out heresy, punish the rebels and impose taxes. It was Philip's worst miscalculation. The highly mercantile Netherlanders then came out against him in open revolt, beginning the 80-year war that gave birth to modern Holland and inflicted on Spain an unstanchable hemorrhage of men and treasure.

Elsewhere, though, Spain was going from strength to strengh. In 1571, a predominantly Spanish fleet smashed Turkey's plan for Mediterranean domination at the Battle of Lepanto. The same year, the conquest of the Philippines, named after the king, was completed with the founding of Manila. And, in 1580, Philip added the crown of Portugal to his own.

Although he was the mightiest potentate in Europe and a great patron of the arts, Philip lived in an ascetic life. He spent most of his time in a spartan little suite inside the huge but austere fortress-cum-monastery of the Escorial, itself some 30 miles from the new capital of Madrid. At the Escorial, he planned the extirpation of the Dutch rebels by eliminating their greatest supporter, Elizabeth of England. But his Armada of 1588 was a failure. As a result of bad weather, bad luck and English harassment, barely more than half

Completed in 1584, Philip II's great palace of San Lorenzo de El Escorial lies 30 miles from Madrid, seen through the haze in the background of this contemporary painting. The rigidly formal building was designed as a monastic retreat where the king could grapple with the problems of empire.

of its ships returned to Spain, their mission unaccomplished. More taxes were extorted from Castile; Aragon, its privileges threatened, flared into brief revolt in 1591. The whole imperial edifice was·clearly in danger of collapse.

Yet, when Philip died in 1598, his son Philip III inherited more territory than his father had and, in the late 16th and early 17th centuries, Spanish society, although financially impoverished, enjoyed one of the richest cultural periods in its history. Appropriately, the greatest writer of the time was Miguel de Cervantes: The absurd and threadbare grandeur of his Don Quixote (protagonist of the novel *Don Quixote)* matched the spirit of the age.

At the turn of the century, Spain was fighting the English, the Dutch, the French and the Turks. Although truces

and treaties brought temporary peace with most of these enemies, the respite was short; the nation was soon drawn into the murderous potpourri of quarrels that became known as the Thirty Years' War.

The weary *tercios,* unpaid, undernourished and often ragged, made up in courage and stubborn honor what they lacked in resources. In 1626, Philip IV could still declare, "We have had all Europe against us, but we have not been defeated, nor have our allies lost, while our enemies have sued for peace." But his boast would not remain true for long. In a brilliant stroke, the Dutch captured the entire treasure fleet of 1628, infuriating the Spanish, even though the flow of wealth had greatly diminished since its peak in the 16th century. In an attempt to rectify

Spain's chronic financial difficulties, the king's chief minister proposed an equalization of military and tax burdens throughout the provinces of the empire, which brought about a revolt of Catalonia in 1640. Portugal broke free permanently in the same year, and in 1643, for the first time, French troops decisively defeated the *tercios* at Rocroi. By the time a disadvantageous peace was finally made with France in 1659, Spain's claim to European predominance was no longer true.

As Spain's power declined and its economic crisis deepened, it turned inward to a deeply Catholic, conservative nationalism, which tended to blame all the nation's ills on outsiders. From 1609 onward, in a move that recalled Ferdinand and Isabella's expulsion of the Jews in 1492, Spain expelled its re-

A suit of ceremonial armor with a life-like portrait head of painted silver was used as a stand-in for audiences by Philip II. The king's reluctance to mingle with his subjects allowed a dangerous breach to develop between his policies and the realities of the country he had to govern.

maining Moors — about 300,000 of them. The gesture could hardly have been more counterproductive: Just as the persecution of the Jews had hampered Spanish commerce, so the banishment of the Moors, who were among Spain's most assiduous farmers, dealt agriculture a grievous and entirely self-inflicted blow.

Throughout the 17th century, the rural population declined, though some cities, especially Madrid, grew. The later Hapsburg kings were each progressively weaker and more inept than their predecessors, and for much of the time, the nation was governed in practice by ministers interested only in self-enrichment and the advancement of their particular factions. Aragon at times threatened secession, and for many years, Catalonia was under French occupation as a result of ceaseless, and pointless, dynastic wars.

And so when, in 1700, Charles II died childless, few people regretted the extinction of the dynasty. Charles had willed the kingdom to his young great-nephew, Philip of Anjou, a grandson of Louis XIV of France. The choice was generally welcomed in Spain, but the idea caused great alarm abroad: If both Spain and France were ruled by Bourbons, it was possible that they might unite under a single crown at some future date. In 1702, Austria, the Netherlands and England declared what came to be called the War of the Spanish Succession.

Catalonia — where the repression that followed the revolt of 1640 was remembered with great bitterness — rose up in arms on behalf of the Austrian Archduke Charles, the alternative to Philip. The conflict therefore became something of a civil war — and provided Philip with the excuse he had

been looking for to extend Castilian centralism everywhere in Spain, except the always fiercely independent Basque provinces.

The war went badly for Philip at first. Madrid was occupied, briefly, by an Anglo-Austrian army; Gibraltar fell to the British, who control the fortress to this day (a fact that continues to strain Anglo-Spanish relations). Yet Philip emerged partly victorious at the Peace of Utrecht in 1713. He had lost most of Spain's remaining European possessions, but he kept his throne. As always, the cost of war had been ruinous, but after the last Catalan diehards surrendered at Barcelona in 1714, it seemed that the Bourbons were at least in control of a united Spain, ready to exploit a long period of peace.

Instead, Bourbon ambitions — and Bourbon disregard for the interests of the people — plunged Spain into another series of futile wars. The concomitant taxation, it was estimated, reduced two million of its eight million inhabitants to subsistence.

Reform of a system strangled by special interests had become an urgent necessity. The process was started by Ferdinand VI, Philip V's successor, who ruled from 1746 to 1759, and continued by Charles III. Land reform and an agricultural revival followed a reorganization of the machinery of central government; and an attempt was made to create a more efficient colonial administration to increase trade with the homeland; new industries sprang up, particularly in Catalonia. Many civil servants were "Regalists," who believed that the Church should confine itself to spiritual matters, leaving control of civil affairs to the Crown. Their main targets were the Jesuits, regarded at the time as the pope's chief support. Conse-

A CHRONOLOGY OF KEY EVENTS

25,000-10,000 B.C. Paintings at Altamira Cave, near present-day Santander, depict the Cro-Magnons' hunt for food.

c. 3000 B.C. The Iberians, a people thought to be of North African stock, start to settle in the south and east of the peninsula to which they eventually give their name.

c. 1000 B.C. Phoenician traders found the city of Gadir — now Cádiz — on Spain's Atlantic coast.

800-700 B.C. Celtic tribes cross the Pyrenees into Spain.

c. 540 B.C. Spain's Phoenician settlements are incorporated into the expanding empire of Carthage, a former colony of the Phoenicians in North Africa.

237-228 B.C. Rivalry with Rome spurs the Carthaginians to widen their hold over the Iberian Peninsula.

218-201 B.C. Rome destroys Carthage's power in the Second Punic War, and the peninsula is later divided into Roman provinces.

392 A.D. The Spanish-born Emperor Theodosius I makes Christianity the only tolerated religion in the empire.

409 Vandal, Suevi and Alani tribesmen invade Spain from the north.

411 The Visigoths enter Spain. After years of conflict with the other Germanic invaders, they eventually establish their ascendancy over the entire Iberian Peninsula, ruling from their new capital, Toledo.

589 Latin Christianity is proclaimed the state religion of Spain after the conversion of King Recared from Arianism, a heretical form of Christianity.

c. 655 A single code — the Libera Judiciorum — gives legal form to the Visigothic state.

711-716 Encouraged by enemies of King Roderick, Muslims from North Africa defeat the Visigoths, conquering all but the northern mountain regions of the peninsula. For the next seven centuries, a Moorish culture flourishes in Spain *(manuscript, left)*.

c. 720 The Christians of Asturias defeat Muslim forces at the Battle of Covadonga, later hailed as the start of the Reconquista — the 700-year campaign to reconquer Muslim Spain.

1094 The Castilian knight, El Cid Campeador — later Spain's national hero — takes Valencia; the Muslims recapture the city after his death in 1099.

1137 The kingdoms of Aragon and Catalonia unite.

c. 1140 An unknown author writes the first great work of Spanish literature — an epic poem about El Cid.

1236-1248 The Christian conquest of Córdoba, Murcia, Jaén and Seville leaves Granada as the only remaining Muslim possession in Spain.

1348-1351 The Black Death — an outbreak of bubonic plague sweeping through Europe — kills up to one third of Spain's population.

1391 The economic and social distress brought on by the Black Death provokes a campaign of persecution against Spanish Jews.

1479 Aragon and Castile are united under the joint rule of Ferdinand and Isabella — "the Catholic Monarchs."

1481 The Inquisition, set up in 1478 to investigate the loyalties of the *conversos* — converted Jews — condemns 16 victims to the stake, providing a foretaste of the religious persecution of the next three centuries.

1492 Granada, the Muslims' last stronghold in Spain, falls to the Christians. Columbus plants the banner of the Catholic Monarchs on New World soil. About 150,000 Jews are expelled from Spain by government decree.

1504 Queen Isabella dies.

1512 Ferdinand annexes Navarre.

1516-1556 Ferdinand is succeeded by his grandson, Charles I, the ruler of the Netherlands and the first Hapsburg on the Spanish throne *(shield, opposite)*. Crowned Holy Roman Emperor as Charles V in 1519, he takes on the self-proclaimed role of "God's standard-bearer," fighting protracted wars against both Protestants and Muslims. During his reign, Spain becomes a leading maritime power and embarks upon the colonization of the Americas.

1521 A Spanish-led force under Hernán Cortés takes the Aztec capital of Tenochtitlan, securing Mexico for Spain *(above)*.

1540 Ignatius Loyola, a former soldier from the Spanish Basque region, founds the Society of Jesus, soon one of the most powerful religious orders in Europe.

1556 Charles is succeeded by his son, Philip II, known as Philip the Prudent.

1561 Philip moves his capital to Madrid.

1563-1584 The huge royal palace, the Escorial, is built near Madrid.

1564 Spain starts to colonize the Philippines, named in honor of the king.

1568-1648 A revolt by the mainly Protestant Netherlanders involves Spain in an 80-year war that ends with the establishment of Dutch independence.

1571 Commanded by Philip's half-brother, Don Juan of Austria, the combined fleets of Spain, Venice and the papacy smash the Turkish navy at the Battle of Lepanto, in the Mediterranean.

c. 1577 The Cretan painter El Greco settles in Toledo (*painting, above right*).

1580 With the annexation of Portugal, Philip temporarily unites the Iberian Peninsula under Spanish rule.

1588 The Great Armada, sent to invade Protestant England, is defeated and largely destroyed.

1598 On the death of Philip II, the crown is passed to his son, Philip III, who rules through court favorites and devotes more time to hunting and the theater than he does to the affairs of state.

1599-1600 A plague epidemic claims some half a million victims in Castile.

1605 Cervantes publishes the first part of his comic masterpiece, *Don Quixote* — a book that is reprinted more often than any other volume except the Bible.

1609-1614 About 275,000 Moriscos (Christianized Muslims) are expelled from Spain.

1621-1700 Unsuccessful wars waged by Philip IV and Charles II cause a further decline of Spanish power. In 1640, Catalonia revolts and Portugal asserts its independence. The painters Murillo and Velázquez add to Spain's cultural heritage.

1700 Charles II, who dies childless, is succeeded by Philip V, a grandson of Louis XIV of France and the first Bourbon to sit on the Spanish throne.

1702-1714 In the War of the Spanish Succession, the Austrians and British attempt to replace Philip V with their own candidate, Archduke Charles of Austria. Although Philip eventually secures his throne, the Austrians take over most of Spain's possessions in Europe, while the British obtain Gibraltar and Minorca. Britain later gives up Minorca but holds onto Gibraltar.

1767 Regarding the Jesuits as a threat to royal supremacy, the reformist king, Charles III, orders their expulsion from Spain.

1793 The execution of Louis XVI by French revolutionaries prompts his Spanish kinsman, Charles IV, to declare war against France.

1793-1805 The French invade Spain, forcing it into an alliance against Britain. The British navy defeats the Franco-Spanish fleet at Trafalgar, destroying Spain's power at sea.

1808-1814 Napoleon, now emperor of France, places his brother, Joseph, on the Spanish throne, igniting a guerrilla war against the French occupation forces. A British army under Wellington intervenes, defeating the French.

1810-1824 Most of the Spanish colonies in South America succeed in winning their independence.

1812 A *cortes* (parliament) meets in Cádiz and proclaims a liberal constitution restricting royal power.

1814-1833 With the French removed from Spain, the crown reverts to the Bourbon claimant, Ferdinand VII. A ruthless exponent of absolute monarchy, Ferdinand abrogates the constitution and tries to destroy his liberal opponents.

1833-1839 A dispute over the succession involving Ferdinand's infant daughter, Isabella, and his brother, Don Carlos (*below*), leads to the First Carlist War. Don Carlos is defeated and leaves Spain.

1839-1868 Popular revolts in the cities and military *pronunciamientos* (officers'

rebellions) overthrow governments of varying shades of liberalism.

1868 A *pronunciamiento* backed by a radical revolt against Isabella's irresponsible rule forces her into exile.

1870-1874 Prince Amadeo of Savoy accepts the Spanish crown, but he abdicates three years later. After further conflicts with the Carlists and a brief period as a republic, the country enthrones Isabella's son, King Alfonso XII.

1898 Spain loses Puerto Rico, the Philippines and Cuba in the Spanish-American War *(cartoon, below)*.

1909 A general strike in Catalonia leads to an outbreak of church-burning and rioting in Barcelona. Brutal repression follows.

1912 A Spanish protectorate is established in northwest Morocco.

1917-1923 An attempt to liberalize the monarchy ends in a socialist-led general strike, which is crushed by the

army. Subsequent anarchist-inspired strikes are also put down.

1921 An attempt by the army to suppress dissident tribesmen in Morocco leads to the massacre of 15,000 Spanish soldiers at Annoual.

1923-1930 Backed by Alfonso XIII, General Miguel Primo de Rivera capitalizes on the increasing weakness of parliamentary government to take over as dictator of Spain. But his policies prove unpopular with both the king and the army, and he is eventually forced to resign.

1925-1927 Spanish and French forces collaborate in defeating Moroccan tribal leader Abd el-Krim.

1931 Faced with an overwhelming republican vote in municipal elections, King Alfonso XIII voluntarily goes into exile. The Second Republic is proclaimed, and a democratic, reformist government is installed.

1933 José Antonio Primo de Rivera, son of the former dictator, founds the Falangist party, modeled on Italy's Fascist party.

1933-1936 The right is returned to power and sets about undoing the previous government's reforms.

1934 The army crushes armed revolts in Catalonia and Asturias.

1936 The Popular Front, an alliance of left-wing parties, wins a decisive majority in general elections.

1936-1939 An attempted coup by right-wing generals leads to the Civil War. General Francisco Franco, heading an insurgent government, triumphs with the aid of Hitler and Mussolini.

1945-1946 Spain is excluded from the newly formed United Nations. The ban is followed by a diplomatic boycott and trade embargo.

1947 The Law of Succession, making Spain a monarchy, is approved in a referendum. It provides for a member of the royal family to succeed Francisco Franco.

1953 In return for generous financial aid, Franco agrees to the siting of four U.S. military bases in Spain.

1955 Spain is admitted to the United Nations.

1956 The Spanish protectorate in Morocco is abolished.

1959 The ETA (*Euzkadi Ta Azkatasuna*, or Freedom for the Basque Homeland), a terrorist group dedicated to winning independence for the Basque provinces, is founded.

1969 Franco chooses Juan Carlos, grandson of Alfonso XIII, as his successor.

1972 Spain signs a trade pact with the Soviet Union.

1973 Franco's newly appointed prime minister, Admiral Carrero Blanco, is blown up in an attack by ETA assassins.

1975 With the death of Franco, Juan Carlos is crowned king.

1976 The Law of Political Reform, re-establishing democracy in Spain, is endorsed by almost 95 percent of voters in a national referendum.

1977 Spain holds its first free elections in 40 years; the center-right forms a government under Adolfo Suárez. Negotiations for membership in the EEC get under way.

1978 A new democratic constitution, guaranteeing civil liberties and autonomy for the regions, is approved in a national referendum. ETA attacks on the security forces result in more than 50 deaths.

1979-1980 The Basques and Catalans are given a wide degree of autonomy. Spain becomes a quasi-federal state, consisting of 17 Autonomous Communities.

1981 King Juan Carlos is instrumental in thwarting an attempted military coup.

1982 Prime Minister Calvo Sotelo negotiates Spain's entry into NATO. A few months later, the Socialists, led by Felipe González, win a landslide election victory.

1986 In a national referendum, voters reaffirm Spain's membership in NATO, on three conditions: that nuclear weapons are banned on Spanish soil, that the United States cut back its troop strength in Spain and that the country be allowed to maintain a separate military.

quently, the order was expelled from Spain and its colonies in 1767.

Although these reforms relieved the country's economic problems and the population rose to 12 million, Spain had no contact with the great surge of ideas of the European Enlightenment. To be sure, the francophile Bourbon court in Madrid shared or imitated many French attitudes, and the nation could claim some far-sighted statesmen, notably Gaspar Melchor de Jovellanos. But few progressive notions permeated ordinary Spanish society, insulated as it was from new ideas by the double censorship of the Inquisition and of the royal authorities. When the French Revolution erupted in 1789, however, Spain's isolation proved impossible to maintain.

Initially, the intelligentsia in Madrid greeted the great revolutionary cry of "Liberty, Equality, Fraternity" with enthusiasm, but after the execution of Louis XVI of France, the people of Spain united behind their king in horror at the godless regicides that were taking place across the border. Yet, when the French invaded Spain in 1792, popular feeling proved to be powerless against the revolutionary armies. A humiliating peace was signed two years later. Spain reluctantly allied itself with France against Britain, setting the stage for the worst national disaster since the Islamic conquest.

In the face of Britain's overwhelming sea power, Spain's transatlantic possessions were essentially indefensible, and the breakup of the Spanish-American colonies began. Worse still, when the imperially minded Napoleon Bonaparte supplanted the Revolutionary government in Paris, France's demands on Spain increased. In 1800, Napoleon obliged Spain to cede him the North American territory of Louisiana. (In 1803, short of cash, he sold it to the United States.) Then, in 1802, he again compelled Spain into war with Britain. As a reward, the Spaniards were to see their fleet destroyed in 1805 at the Battle of Trafalgar.

In 1807, Napoleon — who was emperor by this time — sent troops through Spain to invade Portugal. More troops followed to garrison Spanish cities, angering and bewildering the populace. The next year, Napoleon took more drastic measures, forcing Ferdinand VII, the new king, to abdicate. The emperor's plans for Spain did not include the Bourbons.

In scenes immortalized by the great Spanish painter Francisco de Goya, the population of Madrid rose up against the French. The revolt was crushed with great brutality, and Napoleon installed his brother Joseph as king of Spain. The result was a rebellion that soon developed into what Spaniards call the War of Independence. It was a people's war, considered by some to be the first in history. Spanish regular troops were usually easily beaten by Napoleon's veterans, but victories of the conventional kind were meaningless in a campaign of ambush and assassination, atrocity and counteratrocity. Their struggle gave the world a useful new word: *guerrilla*, a "little war."

In an unlikely alliance between two nations that had spent most of the preceding 250 years at war, the British sent a small army under their most redoubtable general, Arthur Wellesley, later the Duke of Wellington. The combination of a conventional army, skillfully led, and a nation of *guerrilleros*, anxious to kill Frenchmen at any cost, was devastating. At one time, Napoleon deployed 300,000 men against his foes, but they achieved nothing. With good reason, the emperor called the campaign his "Spanish ulcer."

The war was perhaps the cruelest in Spain's history. The Spanish employed a scorched-earth strategy that denied the invaders the supplies they needed but that inflicted equal suffering on their own rural population. French foraging parties were often the victims of merciless ambushes; outposts and stragglers shared the same fate, and French soldiers became familiar with the sight of the mutilated bodies of comrades who had strayed a few yards from the line of march. They reacted with a savagery that shocked the British. Describing how the French sought supplies from an unwilling peasantry, one British officer wrote: "Mothers were hung up with the children by their sides, and fires lighted below them."

Cruelty, however, availed the French nothing. By 1814, the Spanish and British had cleared the country of them and the war was over. Ferdinand returned, to the joyous acclaim of his people, but the monarchy he resumed had changed since 1808. In 1812, leaders of the War of Independence had thrashed out a new constitution for Spain, limiting royal power in favor of an elected *cortes*, or parliament. Although Ferdinand abrogated the constitution and jailed most of its liberal supporters, a rebellion in 1820 forced him to accept it. But — in power once more — the liberals indulged in the ancient Spanish custom of persecuting their enemies until the political pendulum swung the other way and their enemies in turn enthusiastically persecuted them. Thus, the pattern was set for the next century or so of Spanish history: coup and countercoup interspersed with periods of all-out civil war.

2

When Philip IV's court painter Veláz-quez completed his *Ladies in Waiting* in 1656, Spain's golden age was nearing its end. The king — whose five-year-old daughter, Margarita, occupies the center of the picture — died in 1665, leaving an exhausted treasury and a dismembered empire.

Torn by internal dissension and exhausted by the late war, Spain could do little to prevent the secession of its American colonies, which had begun to assert their independence during the years of French occupation of the homeland. By 1824, only Cuba, Puerto Rico and the Philippines remained under Spanish control.

When Ferdinand died in 1833, a six-year civil war broke out over the succession to the throne, with his infant daughter Isabella and his brother Don Carlos as rival claimants. The latter was supported by traditionalists who held that the throne could be inherited only through the male line, and though the Carlists were defeated, the unsurpassed bitterness of the conflict opened chasms of hatred that were not easily healed. Thereafter, the 1812 constitution remained sporadically in force. But its spirit was vitiated by the factional infighting of the liberals, who were only too willing to seek the support of "swords" — generals prepared to back their case by force of arms. The various changes of government that followed were frequently brought about by *pronunciamientos,* or "pronouncements," made by groups of army officers, that were in effect military coups d'état.

Queen Isabella herself proved to be a powerless figurehead. Her popular appeal was compromised by a well-earned reputation for nymphomania ("the queen's terrible constitutional malady," as a contemporary Englishwoman coyly put it), which also cast doubt on the legitimacy of her many offspring.

In 1868, one of the *pronunciamientos* set off something akin to a popular revolution, and Isabella departed for exile in France, to be replaced in 1870 by Amadeo of Savoy, an Italian prince. He abdicated after three years, having failed to resolve the political conflicts, and was followed by a short-lived federal republic. The dust finally settled when Alfonso XII, son of Isabella, was declared king by an army brigadier. In the hope that it would lead to the alternation in power of two political parties on the British model, a new constitution was applied in 1876.

Although the arrangements of 1876 brought Spain a much-needed spell of relative stability, governments of the so-called Restoration Period never really came to terms with Spain's chronic political difficulties. In 1898, when the upstart United States seized, with humiliating ease, what was left of Spain's colonial empire, there was a paralyzing loss of confidence: Spaniards of every class doubted the system's ability to guide Spain into the 20th century. From the first stirrings of an industrial economy, concentrated in Catalonia and the Basque Country, grew a well-organized and politically conscious working class. A socialist labor-union federation, the UGT, was formed in 1882; an even more powerful anarcho-syndicalist union group, the CNT, was founded in 1911. The period also spawned the "Generation of '98" — a group of writers and thinkers that included the novelist and poet Ramón María del Valle-Inclán and the philosopher Miguel de Unamuno — who dedicated themselves to rescuing the nation from its sorry state.

The outbreak of World War I, in which Spain was firmly neutral, created a demand for Spanish steel and other goods that helped to alleviate the economic distress the industrial regions had suffered since 1898. But by 1917, rising prosperity no longer kept up with rising prices. The socialists and anarchists, inspired by the revolutionary events in Russia, were ready to challenge the government. Taking advantage of an ill-defined mood of discontent spearheaded by junior officers striking for more pay and by Catalan nationalists who were demanding autonomy, they launched a general strike. However, the army remained loyal, at least to itself, and the would-be revolutionaries were put down, bloodily. For the next few years, Spain's working-class centers — most particularly Barcelona — were virtually at war with the rest of the country. The military repression cost hundreds of lives; anarchist assassins struck whatever counterblows they could, and employers in turn hired gunmen to kill anarchist workers. Both sides were accumulating painful scores that would not easily be settled.

The political temperature went even higher in 1921, when a colonial adventure in Morocco went dangerously wrong. Since 1909, the Spanish government had been engaged in establishing a protectorate over the section of Morocco not already "protected" by the French. In part it was a compensation for the lost overseas empire, and in part a distraction from problems at home. The policy had misfired even at its inception, when a call-up of reservists had inspired strikes and riots in some cities. Now, however, Spanish military incompetence pitted against determined Moroccan resistance produced a disaster in which almost 15,000 Spanish soldiers were massacred.

News of the defeat rocked not only the government but the whole constitutional system, and left-wingers clamored for retribution. But the army forestalled them. In 1923, General Primo de Rivera put the military beyond public criticism by a *pronunciamiento* that made him dictator of Spain — with the support of the king, Alfonso XIII. It was not entirely a self-seeking move. Primo de Rivera was convinced that a short period of no-nonsense military rule would stabilize the country sufficiently for him to return it to civilian government. Although he managed to defeat the Moroccans, his dictatorship achieved nothing but a sullen truce between Spain's hostile factions. By 1930, he had lost the support of even his fellow generals, and he resigned.

There was no going back to the old system, however. By his support for the dictatorship, Alfonso had discredited the whole idea of constitutional monarchy. In April of 1931, nationwide municipal elections showed overwhelming support for a republic. Without officially abdicating, Alfonso packed his bags and left, like his grandmother before him, for France. The short, tragic history of Spain's Second Republic was about to unfold.

Spain's new constitution declared the establishment of a "democratic republic of workers of all classes," and most of the leaders of its first government shared radical and anticlerical leanings. They promised regional autonomy to provinces that desired it and agrarian reform to solve the age-old problem of Spain's landless peasants. Unfortunately, most of these ambitions were impractical: The abolition of Church control of education, for instance, was all very well, but the Republic had no resources to replace the schools it was abolishing. Nor could the Republican constitution satisfy the anarchists, for whom government of any form was anathema. Soon the government was using force ruthlessly to put down anarchist risings, thus alienating many of its own supporters.

By the elections of 1933, there was enough disillusionment for power to pass to parties of the center and the right, who promptly set about undoing everything their predecessors had accomplished. But the right was scarcely better able to keep order than the left. Strikes were endemic, and in October 1934, something closely resembling a full-blooded socialist revolution broke out. It failed in Catalonia, for want of anarchist support; but in Asturias, thousands of determined miners

2

68

In Goya's painting of the events of May 3, 1808, a French firing squad executes a group of Spanish patriots after an uprising in Madrid against Napoleon's occupying forces. The guerrilla war that followed lasted until 1814, when the French were driven out with the aid of British regular troops.

armed with smuggled weapons and their own dynamite seized almost the entire region. It took naval gunfire, 15,000 troops — including the Spanish Foreign Legion — and two weeks' hard fighting, with heavy casualties on both sides, before the miners were crushed. Significantly, the troops were directed from Madrid by a rising young general called Francisco Franco.

In 1935, a succession of financial scandals involving ministers caused the collapse of the ruling coalition. The Cortes was dissolved and, in the elections of February to March 1936, a newly formed "Popular Front" of leftist parties won a sweeping majority. But their strength in the Cortes was the result of Spain's complex electoral system. Left and right had polled almost equally: The country was split in half.

The Popular Front embraced a wide range of political views, but the forthright Marxism of the socialist leader, Largo Caballero, dominated, with the support of the small but highly organized, and Moscow-controlled, Communist party. In any case, political debate had moved into the streets. Backed by armed militias controlled by the various left-wing parties, mobs howled for the dictatorship of the proletariat; in Barcelona, something like a genuine social revolution occurred. The right wing, too, abandoned what little faith it had in parliamentary democracy and turned to its own armed organizations, especially the mystical, half-Fascist Falange (Phalanx).

For months, senior army officers had been plotting a coup, worried by the inroads leftist propaganda was making on their men. Franco, on the fringes of the conspiracy, counseled caution: Almost alone among the generals, he was convinced an intervention would lead to a long and bloody struggle. But by July 1936, as commander of Spain's troops in North Africa, he was ready to join Generals Sanjurjo, Goded and Mola in a concerted insurrection. The Nationalists — as the group called themselves — hoped to control all of Spain in a matter of hours. In the event, they needed almost three years.

The government could count on the support of more than a third of the army and almost half of the country's various paramilitary police forces, and in most of the important cities, it had the loyalty of armed workers' militias. Thus Madrid, Barcelona and Valencia remained firmly in government hands. Republican sailors had seized most of the navy's ships from their Nationalist officers, so Franco could find no immediate way to bring his North African army, including Moorish and Foreign Legion troops, better trained than the conscripts elsewhere, to the mainland.

The protracted struggle was to rival the War of Independence in bloodshed and horrors. Each side spread atrocity stories about the other, and all too often these were no more than the truth. The Nationalists shot thousands of prisoners suspected of being even remotely opposed to them. The Republicans followed suit, adding the casual butchery of priests and nuns to their score.

If the cruelty of the war was peculiarly Spanish, so was the courage. At the siege of the Toledo Alcázar, for example, the Republicans captured the young son of the surrounded Nationalist colonel. By means of a surviving telephone line, they allowed him to speak to his father. "What is happening, my boy?" the colonel asked.

"Nothing," came the answer, "but they say they will shoot me if the Alcázar does not surrender."

2

"If it be true," the colonel replied, "commend your soul to God, shout *Viva España* and die like a hero. Good-by, my son, a last kiss."

"Good-by, father," said the boy calmly. "A very big kiss." Later, as promised, he was shot.

The war was, in fact, a national catharsis, a bloody purge of hatreds that had festered for generations. There was something profoundly irrational in the sheer ferocity of the violence inflicted by both sides. Perhaps it was best summed up by the mad war cry of one Nationalist leader: "Down with intelligence; long live death!"

The war's future shape, if not its outcome, became clear within the first few days. Territorially, Spain was divided more or less in half, the Republic controlling Catalonia, Valencia, parts of Andalusia, Asturias and the Basque Country. (The staunchly Catholic Basques were prepared to stomach the fervent anticlericalism of the Republic in exchange for the regional autonomy it granted in 1936.) The country was divided in half spiritually, too, as traditional Spain and progressive Spain grappled with each other for their lives.

But the war did not remain confined to Spaniards for long. Nazi Germany and Fascist Italy were both determined to see the right wing triumph. German aircraft helped to ferry Franco's troops to the mainland, and the German "volunteer" Condor Legion contributed to the ground fighting as well as furnishing most of the Nationalist air power. Mussolini also sent troops, while the Italian navy imposed a partial blockade on Republican ports. On the other side of the lines, the Soviet Union supplied the Republic with large quantities of arms and some advisers, but dictator Joseph Stalin did not let his ideological

sympathy cloud his business judgment: His terms were strictly cash, and by the end of the war, some 510 tons of Spanish gold was resting in Moscow vaults.

Not only governments intervened. Spain became the great cause of left-wing idealists all over the world, and volunteers flocked to the so-called International Brigades to fight for the Republic. The largest contingent came from France, though dissident Germans and Italians exiled from their homelands also contributed more than 8,000 men, and there was no shortage of Americans, Poles and Britons of every shade of anti-Fascist opinion.

The net effect of intervention, however, was simply to prolong the war. Gradually, the Nationalists, with German and Italian support, gained the upper hand. The Republic, its back to the wall, indulged in bitter infighting and political purges as the Communists sought absolute power. In a crowning tragedy, thousands of bewildered anarchists, Trotskyites and other political heretics were put to death by Stalinist secret police while the Republic collapsed about their ears. With the fall of Madrid in March of 1939, absolute power in Spain passed to Franco, generalissimo since 1937.

The change of rule had cost more than half a million lives, and more were yet to die as Franco, with the righteous conviction of a 16th-century Inquisitor, set about cleansing the nation. According to some estimates, Nationalist postwar vengeance accounted for more deaths than all the wartime executions of Nationalists and Republicans combined. There was no peace of reconciliation. Instead, Franco adopted the policy of the 19th-century General Narváez. When, as he lay on his deathbed, he was asked to forgive his en-

emies, the old soldier made the classic Spanish reply: "Enemies? I have no enemies. I have had them all shot."

Franco owed much to Hitler and Mussolini, and his right-wing dictatorship was a natural ally of the Axis powers in World War II. Nevertheless, Spain remained officially neutral, despite the considerable pressure from Germany. Franco knew Spain was in no condition for any more fighting, and in any case, he recognized that Nazi Germany, whose barbaric pagan rituals offended his Catholicism, was not likely to be the long-term winner. Spain's dictator was also a hard man to bully: After one negotiating session, Hitler declared, "I would rather have three or four molars out than meet that man again."

Hitler's war with Russia was a different matter. Against the "Bolshevik hordes," Franco contributed the Spanish Blue Division, which lost more than 6,000 men on Germany's eastern front. As the strength of the Allies became apparent, Franco was able to present himself as less pro-Fascist than anti-Communist. After the Allied victory in 1945, Spain was ostracized and was excluded from the United Nations. But as the peace chilled into the Cold War, Franco's anti-Communism was recalled and his pro-Fascism forgotten; by the 1950s, Spain was receiving U.S. aid, and in 1955, it was admitted to the U.N.

Inside Spain, the years from the end of the Civil War to the mid-1950s were difficult. To begin with, there was much hunger, even starvation, while the shattered economy slowly healed. The only permitted political party was the Movement — an amalgam of the forces that had made up the Nationalist side during the war, including the Falange and the Carlists, but reorganized

under Franco's control. As befitted a military dictatorship, there were many spectacular parades; yet these were less in honor of the dictator than of a noble, highly abstract Spain. Franco was the Caudillo, the Leader, but had no intention of founding a dynasty. He had always been a monarchist — it was the flag of the old, royal Spain that fluttered above those parades — but, while he lived, it was obvious that Spain would be a monarchy without a king. Even the adoption in 1969 of young Juan Carlos, a grandson of Alfonso XIII, as prince of Spain and heir presumptive to the title of head of state was a declaration that no change would be permitted — yet.

In fact, Spain *was* changing. The greatest paradox of Franco's 36-year rule was that, beneath a cloak of political stagnation, Spain was evolving faster than ever before in its history, and by the Caudillo's death in 1975, it had been transformed beyond recognition. From a poor, agrarian society, it had become an affluent industrial economy — not yet the match of the rest of Western Europe but gaining fast.

Such changes brought with them inevitable tensions, though the surface order of everyday Spanish life was rarely disturbed. But by 1975, Spain was like a coiled spring held tightly in an iron fist. When Franco died and the fist began to relax, would what followed be a great, invigorating expansion into democracy? Or would the nation simply tear itself apart once more? □

A NATION TORN ASUNDER

The Spanish Civil War was the last and bloodiest act in a drama of social conflict that had been building for generations, setting supporters of a conservative, authoritarian Spain against egalitarians and democrats. After the elections of February 1936 had split the nation almost equally between left and right, a Popular Front government began forcing through a socialist program against the wishes of half the population. But in July, when army generals attempted a coup d'état, they were bitterly opposed by the other half, including some 40 percent of the army itself. The stage was set for 32 months of internecine bloodletting.

The conflict was intensely Spanish in the ferocious blend of heroism and cruelty with which it was fought. But soon it took on an international dimension. At a time when Europe was deeply divided in the prelude to the Second World War, Nazi Germany and Fascist Italy sent troops, tanks and aircraft to help the rebel Nationalist cause; the Soviet leader Stalin dispatched a steady stream of arms and advisers, though no fighting forces, to aid the government-backed Republicans. The plight of Spanish democracy also attracted the attention of liberals and leftists all over the world: 40,000 sympathizers flocked to the country to fight on the Republican side in the volunteer International Brigades.

But foreign aid only served to prolong the war. It was April 1939 before Nationalist leader General Francisco Franco finally ground the Spanish Republic into extinction. By that time, many Spanish cities were in ruins and at least 360,000 men, women and children had died — perhaps a third of them victims of the execution squads set up by both sides. In addition, 500,000 refugees had fled Nationalist vengeance, half of them never to return.

A poster for the film *Espoir* — in English, *Man's Hope* — shows workers illuminated by the sun of the Republican victory they were to seek in vain. The screenplay, taken from André Malraux's novel, was based on the French writer's own adventures as the commander of a volunteer air squadron.

During the battle for Madrid in late
1936, Republican infantrymen hold off
a Nationalist advance in a key mountain pass in the Sierra de Guadarrama
to the north of the capital. The city resisted until 1939.

Near the border post of Irún in the Basque Country, Nationalist troops clear a farmhouse of its Republican defenders. The Nationalists seized the town in September 1936, sealing the frontier with France and isolating the pro-Republican Basque population.

A nattily dressed team of British ambulance drivers poses with its armed escort in a Barcelona street in 1937. In addition to the 40,000 foreigners who fought with the International Brigades, about 10,000 noncombatant volunteers gave much-needed help to the Republic's medical services.

Casually guarded by French colonial troops, hundreds of disconsolate Republican soldiers await an uncertain future in an improvised internment camp just inside the French frontier. In January 1939, during the two weeks that followed the fall of Barcelona, 220,000 survivors from the defeated Republican armies managed to traverse the frontiers before the Nationalists could capture the border crossings. The horrified French at first refused to accept the refugees; eventually, however, they reluctantly granted asylum to Republicans who surrendered their arms. Tempted by a partial amnesty, 70,000 later returned to Spain.

While a helpful French frontier guard carriers her few possessions, a Spanish refugee, in February 1939, offers her poorly clad child what little comfort and protection she can against the icy weather of the Pyrenees.

Safely arrived at the French border town of Le Perthus, an old woman finds less joy in her deliverance than grief for what she has left behind. The journey into exile was an ordeal not everyone survived: Many ran the gauntlet of Nationalist air attacks before finding sanctuary in France.

Their arms outstretched in Fascist salutes, a group of Franco supporters in Barcelona give a frenzied welcome to the Nationalists and their Italian allies, who captured the Catalan capital in January 1939. Most of their fellow citizens, though, were staunch Republicans who found little cause for celebration. Many had already fled into exile; those who remained behind had to endure a five-day looting spree by their liberators, followed by a rigorous repression of all things Catalan. The few remaining Republican leaders were shot, the regional language was proscribed, and even the *sardana*, Catalonia's national dance, was banned.

Flanked by his leading commanders, General Francisco Franco takes the salute at a victory parade in Madrid in May 1939. Unchallenged as Spain's leader — he retained absolute power until his death, more than 36 years later — Franco set about purging the country of "the hatred and passions left us by our past war." To this end, his firing squads worked overtime for months, yet two years later, Spanish prisons were still crammed with almost a quarter of a million prisoners — a convict army that matched in size the battalions marching past the dictator during his Madrid celebrations.

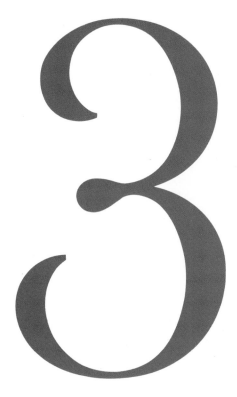

Flanked by bustling thoroughfares, Madrid's 18th-century Palacio Real — formerly the home of Spain's Bourbon rulers — is now used only for state occasions. After the restoration of the monarchy in 1975, King Juan Carlos chose to live in the less ornate Zarzuela Palace on the city's outskirts.

THE ROAD TO DEMOCRACY

For the foreign press, the drama had elements of comic opera. In the early evening of February 23, 1981, the Cortes — the Spanish parliament — had been invaded by rebel soldiers, and now the center of the stage was commanded by a theatrical-looking, mustachioed figure, wearing the quaint, patent-leather tricorn that has distinguished the Guardia Civil since the middle of the 19th century. Standing on the speaker's podium of the Congress of Deputies — the 350-member lower house — he brandished a pistol and boldly proclaimed that he had come to establish a "military government to put an end to terrorism."

But there was no humor in the spectacle for the deputies themselves. They recognized the bizarre figure as Colonel Antonio Tejero Molina, a right-wing fanatic who had been found guilty two years earlier of plotting to capture the entire Cabinet. And if they harbored any doubts about the gravity of his new act of rebellion, these were swiftly dispelled. When General Manuel Gutiérrez Mellado, the white-haired, bespectacled deputy premier, protested at the intrusion, he was struck in the stomach and physically forced back to his seat. Then, at a command from Tejero, his accompanying guards unleashed bursts of submachine gunfire at the balconies, forcing the legislators to duck for cover.

Nor was there any sense of comedy for the millions of Spaniards who witnessed the scene on television or heard it described on the radio. To outsiders, Tejero's style and appearance seemed curiously anachronistic, but to the Spanish people, his sense of mission — to see that the armed forces became the ultimate guardians of the nation's well-being — represented an all too familiar threat. In 200 years, the military had intervened 25 times to become the arbiter of Spain's government. Now, only five years after the death of General Franco, it seemed that Spain's new-founded democracy was in danger of being strangled in its infancy.

The manifold rumors that circulated on that eventful night did little to allay people's fears. This, it emerged, was no isolated action; Tejero had high-level support. One important collaborator was General Jaime Milans del Bosch, the highly decorated commander of the Third Military Region in Valencia, about 185 miles southeast of Madrid. Half an hour before Tejero rushed into the Cortes, the 65-year-old commander had ordered his tanks into the streets and put some 3,500 troops on full alert. Expecting to receive the support of other regional commanders, he then awaited the order to move in force on the capital.

The man he expected to give that command was General Alfonso Armada Comyn, 60, a respected officer of aristocratic background, deputy chief of the army general staff, a former head of the royal military household

3

and a godson of King Alfonso XIII. The rebels envisaged Armada as a leader of sufficient stature to win widespread acceptance of their coup d'état. His critical task was to persuade King Juan Carlos, commander in chief of the armed forces, to proclaim his recognition of a new government.

In the Cortes, Tejero announced that "in about half an hour at most, a competent authority will be coming here." But after an hour, there was no sign of the promised arrival, and soon the parliamentary building was being sealed off by hundreds of loyal armed police. Armada had failed to win the backing of the king. And Milans del Bosch eventually discovered, to his surprise, that he was not being supported by Spain's eight other regional commanders. Shortly before dawn, he ordered his troops back to the barracks.

The following morning, after hours of negotiations, Tejero agreed to surrender. The rebellion had ended in fiasco, and headlines in the popular press labeled it "the crackpot coup." One Socialist deputy, Luis Solana, commented: "The saddest moment was when the implications sank in. But the Spanish people resisted, the institutions resisted. The time of coups is over." More diplomatically, centrist politician Joaquín Garrigues Walker declared: "Thank you, Señor Tejero, for pointing out that our democracy is fragile and incomplete."

In truth, it was premature to talk of Spain's immunity to military coups. The fact was that the rebels had been able to enter parliament with only token resistance and had held it hostage at gunpoint for 18 hours. As legal investigations subsequently revealed, the "crackpot coup" had come closer than was at first imagined to establishing a new dictatorship in Spain. Its failure was due largely to the actions of one man: Spain's new ruler.

When the liberated Cortes resumed business next day, the chamber burst into thunderous applause at the first mention of King Juan Carlos I. Republicans as well as monarchists sustained the fervent ovation. They were recognizing the young monarch as the savior of parliamentary democracy.

For hours while parliament was held hostage, the king, as commander in chief, spoke on the telephone to the captains-general of each of Spain's military regions. Some commanders were slow to pledge their loyalty. Later, Tejero bitterly remarked on the cowardice of opportunist officers who had favored the coup in principle but in practice withheld their support for fear of failure. There may have been truth in his accusation. What is certain is that the king's unequivocal stance finally decided the issue.

At 1:15 a.m. on the night of the coup, Juan Carlos appeared on television to address the nation. In a speech that did much to reassure the public that law and order would prevail, he stated unambiguously: "The crown, symbol of the permanence and unity of the nation, cannot tolerate, in any form, actions or attitudes attempting to interrupt the democratic process." Such an uncompromising posture left even Milans del Bosch — the one conspirator who had made his move — with no choice; as a staunch monarchist, he could not proceed with a rebellion that risked the destruction of the monarchy.

The man most surprised by the king's intransigence was General Armada. Few men had enjoyed a closer relationship with Juan Carlos; Armada had been the king's military instructor in the 1950s and his personal military adviser after he came to the throne in 1975. Yet he, too, blundered, both in anticipating the king's reaction to the army's intervention and in assessing the extent of his political acumen.

It was all part of a familiar pattern. For years, it had been common practice to underestimate Juan Carlos. Cynics tended to see him as a pleasant, rather undistinguished young man, who had achieved his position only through being malleable and unassertive. General Franco had invited him into the professional power game strictly on the understanding that he would conform with, and maintain, the established rules of play. What many Spaniards failed to perceive was that the apprentice had long ago mastered the game and that, in the process, he had developed his own strategy.

As early as 1946, Franco had concluded that a monarchy would be the form of government most suitable for Spain after he relinquished supreme power. Members of the royal family had supported the Nationalists in the Civil War, but Franco had never allowed them to become directly involved in that divisive conflict. Thus, by his intention, the monarchy was the only institution that could legitimately symbolize unity for all Spaniards. It was not intended, however, that the monarchy should interfere with the authoritarian political order he had so firmly established. The man he chose to be king had to be someone prepared to uphold the principles of the Movimiento Nacional, Spain's only permitted political organization, an amalgam of all the different right-wing groups that had supported him in the Civil War.

In 1947, Franco promulgated the

Law of Succession, which decreed that his heir would have the title of king. The obvious candidate as his successor was Don Juan, then aged 34, the acknowledged heir of the last, exiled king of Spain, Alfonso XIII.

Don Juan, however, was regarded by Franco as being too opportunistic for the role he foresaw, and too much influenced by undesirable advisers at his "court" in Estoril, Portugal. The Caudillo was not prepared to sanction his re-turn to Spain for fear that his presence might provide a focus for opposition. At the same time, Franco did not wish to alienate monarchists in Spain by rejecting the prince's claim to the throne. Therefore, he adopted delaying tactics; and in 1948, during long-drawn-out negotiations, he persuaded the royal claimant to have his eldest son, Juan Carlos, educated in Spain.

Juan Carlos was 10 years old when, together with his younger brother, Al-fonso, he first set foot on Spanish soil to attend a special school in San Sebastian with 12 other privileged boys. Holidays were usually spent in the family home in Estoril. (There, in 1956, the future king accidentally and tragically killed the young Alfonso, while loading a revolver given to him at the military academy where he was studying.) Year by year, however, Juan Carlos saw less and less of his father and more and more of Franco who, as a self-appointed guardian, virtually controlled the prince's upbringing in the hope of molding him at last into a suitable candidate for the succession.

In 1961, the 23-year-old Juan Carlos was allowed to take up residence in the Zarzuela Palace on the outskirts of Madrid, not far from Franco's own residence. By now, he had emerged as a young man of some distinction. Besides Spanish, he was fluent in English and French, Italian and Portuguese. He had graduated from the Zaragoza Military Academy third in his class of 271 and had earned a commission in all three services. Yet, for a majority of Spaniards, the tall, gangling youth, stiff and self-conscious in manner, remained an unimpressive figure. His public duties did not go beyond the strictly ceremonial; and in the newspapers and magazines, he was mainly the subject of trivia about his abilities as a yachtsman, a pilot, a judo expert and a radio ham — and of speculation about his marriage prospects.

In Athens, in May 1962, Juan Carlos married his distant cousin, Princess Sofia, the 23-year-old daughter of King Paul and Queen Frederica of Greece. The young royal couple were to have three children: Princesses Elena and Cristina and, in January 1968, a son, Felipe. The birth of a male heir at once enhanced Juan Carlos' status as a future king. One year later, Franco officially named him as his successor, and in the Cortes, the heir apparent formally swore loyalty to the head of state and "fidelity to the principles of the Movimiento Nacional and all other fundamental laws of the realm."

As heir apparent, Juan Carlos was still denied a significant role in the affairs of state. Moreover, his own father refused to recognize his right to the throne. In a statement issued from Estoril but never published in Spain, Don Juan charged Franco with failing to consult the Spanish people in choosing their future monarch.

In November of 1975, when Franco died after having ruled Spain for 36 years, Juan Carlos automatically became the king of a country that was the last dictatorship in Western Europe. Staunch Francoists were still in control of all the major political institutions, and even though the king now had the power to nominate the prime minister, he was restricted by law to choosing from among the three candidates who were proposed by the right-wing Council of the Realm, a 17-man body responsible for advising the head of state on important affairs.

Given this choice, the king could at least have made a change of leadership. Instead, he elected to retain the General's last prime minister, Carlos Arias Navarro — a decision that reinforced the popular belief that Juan Carlos would defend Francoism until the bitter end. In reality, however, the king realized that to support liberal reforms so soon after Franco's death was to risk provoking a coup d'état by the military diehards, even perhaps another civil war. His secret aim was instead to dismantle Franco's institutions by weakening them gradually from within.

The months immediately following Franco's death brought with them a marked relaxation of authoritarianism, for even Arias Navarro realized that some change must come. There was almost total freedom of the press. Demonstrations were allowed, and for the first time since the Civil War, political parties (with the notable exception of the Communists) were permitted to operate openly. But the premier, fearing

Since the implementation of its 1978 constitution, Spain has been a parliamentary monarchy with the king presiding as head of state over a democratic government. The monarch's duties include command of the armed forces, ratification of laws and, on the advice of party leaders, nomination of the prime minister and chief executive, officially titled the President of Government. The president, who takes office only upon a vote of confidence by the Congress of Deputies, appoints a Council of Government to help formulate policy and administer the state.

Spain's lawmakers sit in a bicameral legislature, the Cortes, for terms of four years. Its lower house, the Congress of Deputies, is directly elected from the provinces in proportion to population. In each of the provinces, voters elect four delegates to the Senate, the Cortes' upper chamber. Some senators are also indirectly elected by regional assemblies.

The Congress of Deputies votes on new legislation proposed by the Council of Government or by members of either chamber of the Cortes. The Senate can amend or veto bills passed by the Congress, but the lower house can overturn such actions in a later vote.

Spain is divided into 17 Autonomous Communities, each with a directly elected legislative assembly. Gradually assuming the responsibilities of Spain's previous provincial councils, the assemblies now administer such areas as tourism and environmental protection. A delegate appointed by the national government coordinates regional and state policies.

On the local level, Spain's 8,022 municipalities are run by popularly elected councils. Mayors may be elected either by council members or directly by the citizens.

A CONSTITUTIONAL MONARCHY

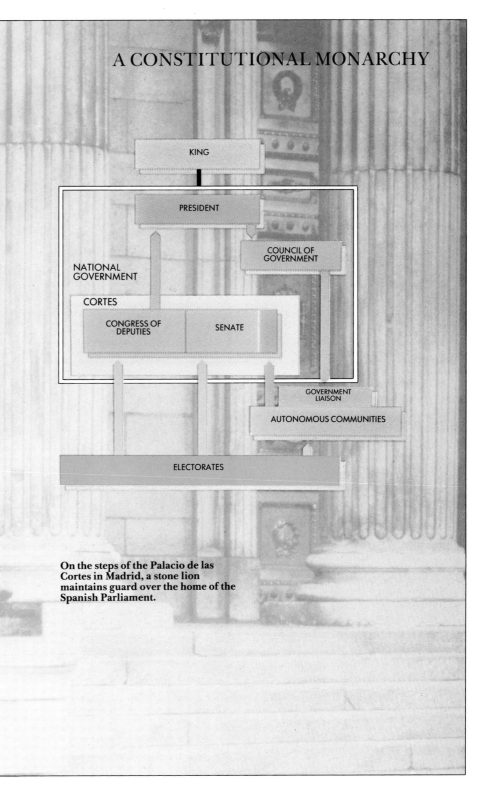

DIRECT ELECTION

INDIRECT ELECTION

APPOINTMENT

KING

PRESIDENT

COUNCIL OF GOVERNMENT

NATIONAL GOVERNMENT

CORTES

CONGRESS OF DEPUTIES

SENATE

GOVERNMENT LIAISON

AUTONOMOUS COMMUNITIES

ELECTORATES

On the steps of the Palacio de las Cortes in Madrid, a stone lion maintains guard over the home of the Spanish Parliament.

3

a head-on clash with orthodox Francoism, failed to make any progress toward constitutional change. Finally, after eight months of the new administration, Juan Carlos asserted his authority: In response to popular demand, he requested the resignation of Arias Navarro. Passing over the more obvious candidates, he named as the new prime minister Adolfo Suárez, a former civil governor and director of Spanish television, who had latterly been Arias Navarro's minister in charge of the Movimiento Nacional.

Again, the king's choice dismayed the majority of Spaniards, who were now clamoring for democratic reforms. Suárez' entire career had been in the service of Francoist administrations. Only 43, he was generally regarded as a political lightweight: an orthodox bureaucrat without sufficient prestige to steer through a program of radical change. Yet this appointment proved to be the king's master stroke. For several years past he had privately sought Suárez' opinion on Spanish politics, knowing him to be an adroit politician, possessed of modern views. As later events showed, Suárez had few ideas for dealing with economic problems, terrorism or labor unrest. But he was a skilled negotiator, and with his intimate understanding of the working of the Francoist power machine, he was supremely well equipped to evaluate the best means of its gradual destruction. Importantly, too, his record was sufficiently conformist not to arouse right-wing opposition when his appointment was announced.

In retrospect, the achievements of the first Suárez administration seem truly extraordinary. Within a year, it legalized political parties, including, most controversially, the Communist

During Spain's 1982 elections, supporters of Fuerza Nueva, or New Force — the far-right party founded by Madrid lawyer Blas Piñar — give the Fascist salute at a rally in Valencia. But neo-Fascist groups failed to gain a single seat in the elections, and Fuerza Nueva was subsequently disbanded.

party. The Francoist syndicates, which fixed wages and determined labor policies, were abandoned after the reestablishment of free trade unions. The Basque flag was legalized. Catalonia was allowed to celebrate its own national day. There were amnesties for hundreds of political prisoners, including leaders of the ETA, who were sent into exile. Most remarkably, in November 1976, the Francoist Cortes was persuaded to vote overwhelmingly in favor of abolishing itself. By passing the Law of Political Reform, the old Parliament agreed to establish a new, bicameral body to be elected by universal suffrage. At the same time, the law abolished the Council of the Realm and so, in effect, made the Movimiento, formerly the sole political party, obsolete.

In June 1977, just 11 months after Suárez' appointment, Spain had its first general election since the onset of the Civil War in 1936. More than 79 percent of the electorate voted. The result was a triumph for Suárez' party, the Union for the Democratic Center (UCD), which attained 34.3 percent of the vote. Felipe González' Socialist party (PSOE) gained 28.5 percent to emerge as the main opposition. Democracy was again a reality in Spain; and, miraculously, it had been restored by using the legal processes of Franco's undemocratic institutions.

The election was, above all, a victory for moderation. The electorate rejected Francoism as represented by the Alianza Popular (AP) party, led by Manuel Fraga Iribarne, a pugnacious conservative who had served under Franco as minister of information and tourism, and, in more recent times, as minister of the interior in the Arias Navarro administration. Almost equally, it rejected the newly legalized Spanish Communist party (PCE), led by the veteran Santiago Carrillo.

Bitterly disappointed by the king's choice of Suárez as prime minister — he aspired to the position himself — Fraga had formed an alliance of former Franco ministers. At a time of international recession, his party hoped to capture the support of the new middle classes that had emerged from the economic boom of the 1960s. Its campaign was fiercely anti-Communist, and it stridently advocated firmer government and stronger enforcement of law and order. But Fraga underestimated the yearning of the electorate for a complete break with the past. In the event, his party polled a mere 8 percent of the vote, gaining only 16 seats in a Congress of 350.

On the left, Carrillo, who had come back to Spain after having spent nearly 40 years in exile, also misjudged the popular mood. In seeking to secure the legalization of the Communist party, he had sworn to support the monarchy and had accepted the nationalist flag. He had also vigorously supported Suárez' reforms and had propounded a form of Eurocommunism that stressed independence of the Moscow line. His party presented a moderate and non-revolutionary image. However, in the 1977 elections, it erred in seeing the Alianza Popular as its main opposition and consequently focused its campaign in the wrong direction. The PCE polled only 9 percent of the vote, winning a mere 20 seats.

In December 1978, some 18 months after the election, Spain's new constitution — approved by parliament and by national referendum — was formally sanctioned by the king. It established a parliamentary democracy with King Juan Carlos I as head of state. Legisla-tive powers were vested in the Cortes, which was to be composed of a lower house (the Congress of Deputies), elected by universal suffrage and proportional representation, and an upper chamber (the Senate) composed of about 250 senators, a majority of them elected directly by the voters of Spain's 50 provinces. It further conceded to every region the right to autonomy, paving the way for Spain's current, semifederal system of 17 Autonomous Communities, each with its own parliament elected by universal vote. Its many other provisions included the abolition of the death penalty and a guarantee of religious freedom.

Much of the credit for the acceptance of the new constitution belonged to the king. He had played a major role in the restoration of democracy by giving unequivocal public support to Suárez, by propagating Spain's growing liberalism in his many meetings with Western leaders at home and abroad, and by maintaining close contact with the military, who needed constant reassurances that liberalization would not automatically lead to disorder and disunity. At the same time, he confounded those who had derisively nicknamed him in advance Juan el Breve (Juan the Brief), expecting his hold on power to be short-lived. The monarchy was now firmly reestablished. One month before the general election, Don Juan had conceded his rights to the throne in favor of his son. And in 1980, centuries of monarchical tradition were restored with the return to Spain from Rome of the body of Alfonso XIII.

By supporting the break with totalitarianism, Don Juan inevitably reduced the monarch's political powers. The constitution now states that the king "arbitrates and moderates the regular

3

working of the institutions." Basically, his governmental duties are restricted to giving his assent and signature to legislation passed by the Cortes. The king summons and dismisses parliament, but only on the recommendation of the prime minister with Cabinet approval. He appoints the prime minister, but only after consultation with the party leaders and the speaker of the Cortes. And the Cortes must give the candidate a vote of confidence by an absolute majority before the appointment can become final.

Nevertheless, the political role of Juan Carlos I far exceeds that of other Western monarchs. To a degree, it is an intangible force that derives from his unique position as the fulcrum of Spanish unity. He has consistently stressed his determination to be "king of all Spaniards"—a resolve exemplified in February 1981, when, in defiance of terrorists' threats and the counsel of his security advisers, he went ahead with the first royal visit to the Basque Country since 1929. Importantly, too, he has made himself a "people's monarch" by his relative simplicity of style. Eschewing the courtly pomp and ceremony of his ancestors, he has declined to move from the two-story, red-brick Zarzuela Palace to the chilly grandeur of the labyrinthine Royal Palace, the traditional home of Spanish kings, and every year he and Queen Sofia undertake hundreds of public engagements with a minimum of formality. His prestige and popular appeal are now so broadly based that political leaders consult him to an extent unknown in other monarchical democracies.

Above all, the king derives power—and awesome responsibility—from his role as the commander in chief of the armed forces. Other Western monarchs hold this position as ceremonial figureheads. Juan Carlos, in contrast, is a working commander, giving as much as one third of his time to military affairs, joining in maneuvers and maintaining very close contact with the service chiefs. As was demonstrated by the aborted coup of 1981, the king's influence with the military establishment can be absolutely critical in a country with a constitution that recognizes the special responsibility of the armed forces to "guarantee the sovereignty and independence of Spain and to defend her territorial integrity and the constitutional order."

Federico García Lorca, the Spanish poet murdered by Franco supporters in 1936, once observed that "the dead in Spain are more alive than in any other country." It is certainly true that the ghost of the Caudillo lingers on like a living presence within the nation's military institutions. For 40 years, the armed forces were the main pillar of Franco's regime. Now, long after his death and Spain's emergence as a parliamentary democracy, the military continues to represent a significant, if now much weakened, factor in the political life of the nation.

Franco's style of government was always militaristic in character, and while under his supreme command, the forces were imbued with a profound sense of mission as the chosen defenders of Spain's traditional values, of a powerful central government and, above all, of national unity—a concept with almost mystical overtones. For decades, without any major international conflict to distract them, a hugely over-manned officer corps was predominantly concerned with fulfilling its clearly defined duty of guarding the nation against communism, separatism, and any other challenge to central authority and law and order.

Proud of their historic role, Spain's military commanders have repeatedly resisted attempts to reform their hierarchy, organization and privilege. In recent years, they have often resisted in vain. Moreover, grudgingly, they have had to accept government legislation in conflict with their basic doctrines—most notably, the legalization of the Spanish Communist party and the granting of a wide degree of autonomy to the regions, especially the Basque Country and Catalonia. Nevertheless, the military establishment is still only partially reformed, and many of its senior officers remain deeply nostalgic for the Franco years, even though they were themselves too young to have fought on the side of the Nationalists during the Civil War.

The tenacity of such conservatism is partly explained by the isolation of the military from civilian life. Many service families live in self-contained communities, the wives doing their shopping in military-run supermarkets and the children attending military schools. A high proportion of officers are married to daughters of other officers, and it is estimated that at least 80 percent of the officer corps is composed of sons of former officers or noncommissioned officers. The generation gap, so conspicuous elsewhere in Spanish life, is thus relatively narrow, and respect for traditional values still remains very much in evidence.

No armed force in Spain is more conscious of its duty to preserve those values than the 63,500-strong paramilitary Guardia Civil, which has the slogan *Todo por la Patria* (All for the Fatherland). Ever since it was formed in 1844,

In Madrid, a half-stripped wall poster
offers the bizarre sight of a headless
Karl Marx carrying a copy of his mas-
terwork, *Das Kapital*. The reappear-
ance of political placards was one of
the first signs of burgeoning democracy after the death of Franco.

Armed with submachine guns, masked ETA terrorists patrol a remote area of the Basque Country as part of their commando training.

A mural protests France's and Spain's thumbs-down denials of Basque independence.

Since Roman times, the Basques of northern Spain have fought against successive rulers to preserve their independence. When Franco tried to assimilate the region, the struggle turned violent. Euzkadi Ta Azkatasuna (Freedom for the Basque Homeland) was formed as a separatist organization in 1959. Two years later, the ETA began an armed campaign, resulting in more than 500 deaths by bomb and bullet.

With the coming of democracy after Franco's death, state policy changed radically and many of the ETA's original demands were met. Basques now have their own parliament, along with the right to fly their national flag and teach their language in schools. Yet the ETA has refused to renounce terrorism, demanding total independence and closer political links with the 250,000 Basques in southwest France, and the killings continue.

with the purpose of suppressing marauding bandits throughout the country, the corps has been an efficient — if sometimes brutal — internal security force for the central government in Madrid. Its basic function is police work: combating crime and enforcing the law in rural areas and in towns with populations of less than 20,000. It is also the nation's principal intelligence-gathering organization. Yet it is part of the Spanish army, and its most important military-style operations are in the Basque Country, where it serves as the government's prime antiterrorist arm, commanded by officers who still believe that the very notion of regional autonomy poses a fundamental threat to the unity of the Spanish state.

To enforce law and order in large urban areas, Franco created a second paramilitary force, the Policía Armada, commonly known as the *grises* because they used to wear all-gray uniforms. The force included riot squads, which earned a reputation for unnecessary violence in breaking up political and labor demonstrations. But in recent years, democratic governments have sought to soften the popular image of the Policía Armada. It has been given a new name — the Policía Nacional — re-equipped with brown uniforms and increasingly removed from military command. In 1983, for the first time, the national police did not take part in the annual Armed Forces Day parade. These services supplement the municipal police, responsible for carrying out a variety of everyday duties, such as traffic control.

Before Tejero's aborted coup, the Suárez government had adopted conciliatory tactics in dealing with the armed forces and the police. Its fear of the military was most strongly evinced in January 1980, when it was discovered that General Luis Torres Rojas, commander of the crack Brunete Armored Division stationed just outside Madrid, was planning a coup. No trial ensued. Discreetly, Torres Rojas was posted some 375 miles away, to be military governor of La Coruña. In contrast, Miguel Angel Aguilar, the editor of the newspaper *Diario 16*, which had exposed the plot, was arrested and forced to resign. Earlier, in 1978, three actors and an actress from a Catalan mime troup called Els Joglars (The Minstrels) had been jailed for two years for "insulting the armed forces" by staging a mime play about an execution under the Franco regime.

After the Tejero affair, the UCD government — which, following the resignation of Suárez because of party faction-fighting, was now led by Leopoldo Calvo Sotelo — was all the more wary of provoking the disapproval of right-wing officers. It scaled down its plans for regional autonomy and introduced tougher antiterrorist measures. Meanwhile, the king warned that it would be "counter-productive" at this stage to crack down too harshly on the armed forces. "Everyone," he said, "must be aware that the king cannot and must not, on his own direct responsibility, repeatedly confront tension and gravity." In effect, Juan Carlos was recognizing that the crisis had almost exhausted his credit with the military, and that, alone, he was not able to guarantee the preservation of democracy.

One year after the attempted coup, 32 officers and one civilian appeared before Spain's Supreme Court of Military Justice to face charges of "military rebellion." The trial highlighted the division between Spain's traditionalists and progressives. The former saw the defendants as heroes who had honorably performed their patriotic duty to protect their country from civil disorder and disunity. The latter regarded them as enemies of democracy who were guilty of terrorism in their own right. On the one hand, Madrid's far-right newspaper *El Alcázar* hailed Tejero as *un valiente* (a man of courage), and officers' messes took up collections for his defense. On the other, politicians of the left and center deplored the fact that rebels against the state should be tried by an all-military court. (After Tejero's previous coup attempt, military judges, though finding him guilty of sedition, had imposed only a seven-month suspended sentence and had allowed him to retain his full rank.)

This time, Tejero and Milans del Bosch were to receive the maximum sentence demanded by the prosecution — 30 years each. Armada was condemned to six years' imprisonment. Other sentences ranged from one to six years, and 11 defendants, mostly junior Guardia Civil officers, were acquitted on the ground that they were obeying orders from their superiors. The sentence on Milans del Bosch was imposed despite his exceptionally distinguished service record. (He had taken part in the legendary defense of Toledo's Alcázar fortress in 1936 and had served in Franco's renowned Blue Division on the Russian front in World War II.) Even so, many politicians protested that the military judges — all senior generals or admirals — had been far too lenient. New legislation was subsequently passed, by which the judgments of a court-martial could be appealed to the civilian Supreme Court, and this procedure was applied in the case of Tejero and his co-conspirators. As a result, eight of the acquittals were

reversed and 22 sentences were increased — in Armada's case, to the maximum 30 years.

Other army reforms have been effected by post-Franco governments. In 1978, for the first time since the Civil War, a civilian defense minister was appointed. That same year, new regulations made military service a full-time occupation; no longer would officers be able to finish work at about midday and take a second, nonmilitary job in the afternoon.

From late 1981 onward, the pace of change was accelerated. Compulsory retirement at 65 was introduced, and promotion examinations were made more demanding. The government announced that it aimed to reduce the strength of the services by more than one third before 1990. Then, in 1982, the UCD government fulfilled its promise to make Spain the 16th member of the NATO alliance. Membership, it was argued, would bring greater urgency to the task of modernizing the forces; and it was the cherished hope of the politicians that it would result in the services becoming more preoccupied with truly military affairs.

The negotiation of Spain's entry to NATO was the last major achievement of the centrists of the UCD. It had always been a loose amalgam of political groups, rather than a cohesive party. Once its primary task of establishing democracy was accomplished, it fell apart, dissolving into a number of lesser political groupings. In the 1982 national elections, a new political force came to the fore: the Spanish Socialist Workers' party (PSOE), under the leadership of 40-year-old Felipe González.

The Socialists won an overwhelming victory at the polls, gaining 43 percent of the popular vote and a 64-seat majority over the combined representatives of all the other parties in the Congress of Deputies. They did so with a program that was essentially centrist, offering nothing more radical than a plan to nationalize the electricity grid and the promise of a referendum on

Spain's continued membership in NATO. Other provisions included reducing the age of retirement for employees from 65 to 64, increasing the length of paid vacations from four to five weeks, indexing pensions to inflation, creating an ombudsman, legalizing abortion and introducing a law on conflict of interest in public-sector jobs. Their moderate reformism, combined with the personal appeal of the youthful, handsome and energetic González, made them the first government of the left since the outbreak of the Civil War.

Significantly, the forces of undiluted Francoism were totally rejected in the 1982 elections. They were chiefly represented by Fuerza Nueva (New Force), a neo-Fascist party founded by Blas Piñar, a Madrid lawyer who had long opposed the democratization of Spain. Having failed to gain a single seat in Congress during this election, however, the party was later disbanded.

Another, more bizarre, representative of the extreme right was the irrepressible Colonel Tejero. While in confinement, he was nevertheless able to organize a political party, Solidaridad Española (Spanish Solidarity). The party nominated a number of candidates, including Tejero himself, and also his son and his daughter. Displaying the highest regard for democratic rights, the Spanish courts declared Tejero's candidacy to be legal. But Solidaridad Española, too, failed to win even a single seat. Tejero himself gained only a tenth of the votes necessary to secure a place in Congress and, with it, parliamentary immunity.

The 1982 general election also brought a resounding defeat for the extreme left. Communist support fell to 4 percent, yielding a derisory four seats. The result reflected a malaise in the Spanish Communist party itself. Membership had slumped from 240,000 to 80,000, and there were deep policy divisions. By now there was a clear trend toward two-party politics in Spain.

The main opposition group that emerged from the elections was the Alianza Popular party, which won 106 seats — a spectacular advance on its earlier showings of 16 seats in 1977 and nine seats in 1979. Its performance at the polls in the 1982 race established the AP as the clear alternative to the PSOE as a potential party of government. The AP could no longer be regarded as the party of Francoism. Since 1977, while remaining under the leadership of Fraga Iribarne, it had shed most of its prominent *franquista* names. It had accepted the basic tenets of Spanish democracy and had been successful in its attempts to broaden its appeal. But the party remains unequivocally conservative in character, standing for strong law-and-order enforcement, the defense of national unity, the maintenance of the free market economy, the reintroduction of capital punishment and freedom of education.

Above all, the Alianza's appeal was based on a return to traditional values. It presented itself as the party for those worried by the pace of change in Spain. It stood for social conservatism and the protection of family life. As such, it was the natural ally of another enduring prop of Spanish life that, like the armed forces, had seen its fortunes in flux since the death of General Franco: the Catholic Church.

On October 31, 1982, the arrival of Pope John Paul II at Madrid's Barajas Airport generated scenes of emotional intensity surprising even for a nation as staunchly Catholic as Spain. Throughout John Paul's 10-day tour, crowds gathered by the hundreds of thousands to accord him a tumultuous welcome. This was, after all, the first time a pontiff had visited the country that had made Roman Catholicism the state religion almost 14 centuries earlier and that, more than any other, had vigorously sought to establish the Catholic faith in other lands. How ironic, then, that such a historic visit should come at a time when the influence of the Church in Spain was in sharp decline, and when the divide between Church and State had become clearly defined.

Though strong, devout and conservative by any standard, the Catholic Church of Spain had experienced a dramatic fall in attendance and in vocations to the priesthood since the late 1950s, when economic growth began to foster a more materialistic society and encourage a massive movement of people from rural areas to the great centers of industry and commerce. At the time of John Paul's visit, about 95 percent of the population remained nominally Catholic; the overwhelming majority of citizens had been baptized in the Church and continued to observe all its rituals associated with rites of passage — weddings, funerals and so forth. But fewer than 30 percent of Spaniards regularly attended mass, and in large cities the figure was nearer 10 percent.

To a certain extent, the decline in the influence of the Church paralleled that of the military establishment. It was a sector of the army that had triggered the Civil War in 1936, and the Catholic Church that had sanctified the conflict — in the words of the then-primate of Spain, Cardinal Isidro Gomá y Tomás — as "a crusade against the godless." After the victory of the Nationalists, the three main pillars of the Franco

93

regime were the armed forces and the Church, together with the Movimiento. Indeed, under the Caudillo, the Church acquired a position of authority that it had not had since the 17th century. Its bishops, like high-ranking military officers, sat in the Cortes and on the Council of the Realm, and once again the Church controlled education and acted as the arbiter of public morality.

All the anticlerical legislation of the Republic was repealed. Marriage was again an indissoluble institution (divorces granted during the Republic were ruled to be invalid); adultery was a crime punished by imprisonment; contraceptives were banned; films, plays and books were all subject to the most rigid censorship. Ecclesiastical influence was further extended in 1953, when Spain and the Vatican signed a concordat that formally recognized the Catholic Church as the Church of Spain. Thereafter, all other religious organizations were forbidden to worship publicly or to advertise services that they held.

In 1962, however, Vatican Council II endorsed the need to separate church from state, and consequently the Church hierarchy in Spain began to distance itself from the regime, a gradual process greatly accelerated following the appointment in 1969 of the liberal Cardinal Vicente Enrique y Tarancón as Archbishop of Toledo and Primate of Spain. Cardinal Tarancón, above all other churchmen, played a critical role in withdrawing the Church from Spanish political life and in supporting the restoration of democracy. In the meantime, to the left, radical clergymen, many of them Jesuits, were active in reestablishing links with the anti-Francoist opposition by forming neighborhood committees and by helping the illegal trade unions.

Within the regime, an important contribution to the modernization of Spain was made by members of Opus Dei (The Work of God), a brotherhood of committed Catholics, both lay and clergy, which had been founded in 1928 by an Aragonese priest, José María Escrivá de Balaguer. Opus Dei is distinguished from other religious orders by the fact that its lay members, sworn to secrecy and obedience, are encouraged to use their individual talents to reach positions of influence, especially in university, commercial and political life. In the 1960s, members achieved great prominence in both commerce and government; indeed, they were the chief technocrats behind Spain's spectacular economic advance. With few exceptions, they were to the right of the political spectrum, but they were committed to efficiency and good management even at the risk of upsetting vested interests.

In 1969, however, the image of Opus Dei was tarnished by the "Matesa Affair." Customs officials discovered that Matesa, a Barcelona-based textile company, had improperly used for private investment abroad credits of up to 10 billion pesetas (about $80 million) granted by the government. It was the greatest financial scandal in Spanish history and resulted in the sacking by Franco of five government ministers, three of them members of Opus Dei.

Since the reestablishment of democracy, the organization has ceased to be a significant political force, and in seeking to preserve conservative orthodoxy in Catholicism, it is, like the Church as a whole, striving to hold back a seemingly irresistible tide of social change. As the British writer Robert Graham observed

Dramatically sited in mountains northwest of Barcelona, the 1,000-year-old Benedictine Monastery of Montserrat is a bastion of Catalan culture. When the Catalan language was proscribed by Franco, its monks defied the ban by conducting weddings and issuing publications in the forbidden tongue.

3

in 1984: "The traditional context in which Catholicism has been rooted in Spain has altered irreversibly. An isolated, inward-looking agrarian society permitted the Church to exert a formidable influence over Spaniards. The Church's implacable insistence on the exclusivity of the Catholic faith and the persecution of heretics reflected a political need to forge unity in a divided nation that had once been dominated by Islam. Catholicism still helps define the nature of Spain. But the unity of the nation is based on a complex interplay of regional interests, economic and social factors, and international relations; they depend little on religion."

The new Spain that has emerged from the political changes since the death of General Franco is outward-looking. Every year, millions of Spaniards take vacations abroad, while millions of foreign tourists descend on Spain. The impact of foreign influence is evident everywhere: in mushrooming bingo halls and discotheques, in pop music, avant-garde fashions (Spain even had its punk rockers by the mid-1980s), television soap operas and, above all, in a more relaxed attitude toward sex.

In the 1940s, public swimming pools were restricted to separate sessions for men and women, and in the 1950s tourists were arrested for wearing bikinis. Now, topless bathing is the norm on most Spanish beaches, and total nudity is allowed in designated areas. Under Franco, the censors denied the slightest suggestion of eroticism in films, plays and books. Now, pornography is a minor industry, and Spaniards can see such controversial films as *Last Tango in Paris* or *The Night Porter* late at night on television. A few decades ago, courtship was universally governed by the code of the *noviazgo,* the tradition whereby a young man (*novio*) cultivates the acquaintance of his chosen sweetheart (*novia*) under strict family and community supervision. Now, at least in the cities, the opposite sexes are able to mingle freely.

The new permissiveness reflects a fundamental change in official attitudes since Franco's day. The sale of contraceptives, and the diffusion of information about them, was permitted in 1978. Divorce was legalized in 1981. Two years later, legislation was passed that allowed abortions in the case of rape, when the fetus showed signs of abnormality or when the health of the mother was seriously endangered. Although the new law's constitutionality was subsequently challenged in the Supreme Court, few people doubted that the measure would eventually be accepted in some form.

Such measures were introduced in the face of open opposition from the Church, and the successful passage of most of them into law marks the ebbing of Catholic influence. But no Spanish government can afford to disregard the views of the Church totally. In the mid-1980s, for example, the Socialist administration chose, in the face of widespread public hostility and mass demonstrations, to compromise over the principle that the country's private schools should be self-financing. Catholic private educational establishments account for a quarter of all kindergartens and more than 20 percent of primary and secondary schools. The Church controls four of Spain's 33 universities, among them the influential University of Navarre, run by Opus Dei. The complete withdrawal of state subsidies to these institutions would seriously undermine the Church's

Teenagers receive a geometry lesson at a school run by Augustine fathers in Madrid. Roughly a third of Spanish children are privately educated, and about 1 child in 6 attends an educational institution run by the Church.

most important area of influence.

Nor has the new moral climate gone unchallenged. The possibility of a backlash against permissiveness has increased, especially since the rising unemployment of the 1980s has brought with it an alarming increase in violent crime and drug abuse — an epidemic that in 1984 impelled the socialists to reverse an earlier attempt to limit narcotics prosecutions to dealers rather than users. Inevitably, this trend has aroused a fresh outcry from those who still look back with nostalgia on the disciplined social order that was imposed under the Franco regime.

Yet, by the mid-1980s, few people sought a return to the politics of Francoism. In many respects, Spain was a different land from the one the Generalissimo had ruled. The most tightly centralized of nations now had local parliaments, bringing an unprecedented degree of autonomy to the administration of its 17 regions. The most Catholic of nations now recognized in its constitution the separation of church and state. In June 1985, a further step was taken toward safeguarding the democratic way of life when, after eight years of negotiations, Spain, together with Portugal, finally signed the treaty of accession to join the other 10 democracies of the European Economic Community.

Three times before, in 1962, 1966 and 1970, Spain's application for association with the EEC had been rejected on the grounds that the country was not a true democracy. Now the break from Francoism was given international recognition. As Spain became fully integrated into the Western European socioeconomic structure, the prospect of a return to authoritarianism seemed to become increasingly unlikely. □

An elderly citizen salvages food scraps from the remnants of a street market in the city of Leon. The government provides social-security benefits for less than a third of Spain's unemployed, who, by early 1986, represented almost 22 percent of the work force.

Fresh from the assembly line, rows of
gleaming Opel Corsas stand in the
grounds of the General Motors factory
at Saragossa in northeast Spain. Auto
manufacturing helped pioneer Spain's
industrial leap forward in the 1950s;
by the 1980s, the country had become
the fourth-largest producer in Europe.

THE TAKE-OFF YEARS

If asked which European country had enjoyed the fastest rate of economic growth during the decade and a half from 1955 to 1970, few people would give the correct answer: Spain. Yet during the late 1950s and the 1960s, the Spanish economy grew at the unprecedented average annual rate of 7 percent, double that of West Germany and only slightly less than that of Japan. Like the experiences of those two nations, Spain's achievement has been dubbed a miracle, and in many ways it was more unexpected. Both Germany and Japan were already important industrial powers before global war devastated their economies; Spain, however, was still essentially an agrarian, underdeveloped country in the first half of the 20th century.

By the time General Franco took over in 1939, the Industrial Revolution, which had transformed northern Europe in the last century, had scarcely begun to filter across the Pyrenees. Nearly half of Spain's active population worked the land. In the aftermath of the Civil War, this proportion was swollen still further when hunger and unemployment in the cities forced many Spaniards to return to their villages. A dry climate and poor soil meant that most of the country's fields offered a hard living at best. Even such naturally favored areas as Andalusia and Galicia had problems. Inefficient systems of land tenure — in Andalusia, great *latifundios*, or tenant farms, owned by ab-

sentee landlords, in Galicia, the endless subdivision of plots — hindered progress. In other fertile regions, farmers could not invest in new methods and machinery to increase productivity because credit was difficult to get except at extortionate rates from landlords.

Franco himself was obsessed with the goal of self-sufficiency, but his regime's attempts to boost productivity were disastrous. In 1937, the Servicio Nacional del Trigo (the National Service for Wheat), which was charged with guaranteeing wheat prices by buying up, storing and selling the entire harvest, set off the worst fiasco to beset Spanish agriculture. In fact, the bureau's main achievement, besides discouraging the growing of profitable export crops such as citrus fruits, was to encourage a thriving black market. Between 1939 and 1950, the black market accounted for more than half of all wheat sales in Spain. In the famine year of 1945, some cerealgrowers officially declared the failure of their entire wheat harvests — and collected nearly 10 times the set price by selling privately.

Few people benefited from this corruption, and incomes for the majority of the rural population remained low — too low to stimulate the demand that industry needed before it could build production. In 1939, only 20 percent of the work force was engaged in manufacturing, which was concentrated in the north. The other important industrial center was around Barcelona, where a thriving textile business had grown up in the late 19th century. At the turn of the century, heavy industry had been attracted by coal and iron deposits and fast-flowing mountain rivers found in the two coastal provinces of the Basque Country and Asturias. Early investment and technology came from Great Britain, Spain's most important customer during World War I, when such strategic materials as wolfram, mercury and copper were in great demand.

Yet it was precisely these better-off and mainly Republican areas that suffered most during the Civil War. The factory buildings were spared the destruction that would be inflicted on most of northern Europe during World War II, but the civil strife wreaked havoc with the country's industrial infrastructure. Transporation of supplies in Spain was poor to begin with, and the war almost severed these links completely, claiming nearly half of the country's rolling stock and a third of the merchant marine. In addition, half a million dwellings were destroyed or damaged.

Furthermore, the war forced between 350,000 and 450,000 Spaniards into exile. Many of the expatriates were the people who were needed to bring about Spain's modernization — its skilled workers, technocrats, engineers, teachers and lawyers. Although some were eventually to return to Spain, many others made homes elsewhere, in Europe or Latin America. Those Republicans who did remain found themselves subjected to economic and political sanctions.

Franco's own economic ideology had evolved from his conception of a centralized, corporative state. He established a bureaucratic system to control most aspects of the economy, including wages, prices, agricultural yield and the exchange rate. Just as he dreamed of a Spain self-sufficient in food, so he hoped to make Spanish industry free from the vicissitudes of international business. One of his principal organizations was the Instituto Nacional de Industria (INI), which was established in 1941 to industrialize the nation in order to increase military strength and make the country less dependent on imported raw materials.

The INI had its successes. Companies set up to build power stations that used low-grade coal and harnessed the hydroelectric power of rivers in the Pyrenees helped reduce electricity costs for industry. Unfortunately, such projects were few. More typical of INI's track record was a venture to manufacture synthetic fibers that did not produce a significant amount of cellulose for almost a decade. Another undertaking took the same amount of time to conclude that rayon could not be produced from wheat straw.

During the Second World War, when Spain might have expected to profit from its wary neutrality, economic output continued to decline. Exports of cotton goods were down by half compared with the early 1930s; exports of minerals, oranges, wine and olive oil had fallen off by 75 percent. The balance of payments was saved from lurching terminally into the red only because imports had also dropped significantly. Purchases of coal, for example, reached only 12 percent of their average figure before the Civil War.

Throughout the 1940s, the index of industrial production remained below the level it had reached during its peak year of 1929. Agricultural production and national income similarly lagged.

One reason Hitler never marched into Spain was purportedly because he was concerned about the prospect of having to take responsibility for its impoverished population.

For a time after the defeat of Mussolini and Hitler, when Franco's pro-Axis attitude was punished with political ostracism by the international community, widespread starvation seemed possible. The United Nations vote of November 1946 to institute an economic boycott of Spain was not removed until 1953. It was followed in April 1948 by a decision of the U.S. Senate and House of Representatives not to include Spain in the European Recovery Program, better known as the Marshall Plan. Without loans that eventually amounted to $264.3 million from the Peronist government in Buenos Aires, the health of many Spaniards would have been permanently damaged by undernourishment. As it was, the 1940s have come to be remembered bitterly by those who lived through them as "the hungry years."

When change did finally come, it owed less to the efforts of the regime than to rapid political and economic developments taking place outside Spain. By 1950, Cold War tensions were running high, and the United States, alert to the possibility of a Communist backlash in an economically crippled Spain, approved the first of many loans to a regime that at least had impeccable anti-Soviet credentials. This boost was followed in 1953 by the U.S.-Spanish Defense Support Program, whereby the United States government paid more than $600 million in aid and in return was allowed to set up a number of military bases on Spanish soil. More American assistance followed, with the

United States disposing of its agricultural surpluses cheaply to friendly powers. Although the amount of U.S. aid to Spain in the mid-1950s is often overestimated — in total it was less than that allotted to Tito's Yugoslavia — it nonetheless marked a watershed in Spanish affairs, for it ended the country's diplomatic isolation. Further progress came in 1955, when Spain was admitted to the United Nations; three years later it became a member of the International Monetary Fund.

Ironically, one of the greatest stimuli to Spain's development was produced by another exodus of its citizens — this time spurred by the fast-expanding economies of northern Europe. Lured by wages several times what they could earn at home, huge numbers of Spaniards emigrated to Germany, France and Switzerland to take jobs as factory workers, waiters or domestic servants. According to one estimate, 1.73 million people left the country between 1959 and 1973 — a level of emigration that absorbed one third of the annual increase in the working population. Unlike the earlier political refugees, the new emigrants remained close to their roots (more than half eventually returned to Spain) and sent back money to their families or to their savings accounts. In the 1960s, such remittances amounted to $350 million a year, a figure equivalent to 20 percent of the value of Spain's exports.

A substantial number of Spaniards have, then, experienced two forms of exile, the first political and the second economic, in the course of their lives. Raquel Piquer Alsina, born into a Republican Barcelona family in 1934, first traveled abroad as an infant refugee in 1939. Her father, a socialist accountant, was killed that year, and her mother

4

took her across the French frontier to Toulouse. There, the widow married her brother-in-law, Ricardo, a cabinetmaker, who joined the French Resistance and fought the Germans in Vichy territory until they retreated north. The family returned to Spain in September 1944, but Ricardo was denounced as a leftist to the Guardia Civil and sentenced to a term of imprisonment. The next few years were hard for the family. To provide for their needs, Raquel started work at the age of 14 as a secretary in a metallurgical company.

"I was paid 140 pesetas a week," she recalls. "The company was supposed to make parts for machines and marine engines, but there was no metal available in Spain. I decided to study accounting at night school, but it was hard to pay for that out of my wages."

Things improved in 1952, when she got a job working for the director of a film distribution company in Barcelona. Four years later, however, her sister, Carmen, fell desperately ill. Since the family had no money to pay for doctors and there was no social security available, Raquel went to work as a nanny in Switzerland and sent money home for Carmen's treatment. Her efforts were in vain; when her sister died, Raquel returned home.

At the same time that people like Raquel were going abroad to earn the money for life's necessities, the peoples of northern Europe were beginning to identify Spain with the good life of leisure and vacations. The country had magnificent beaches. Land prices for tourist development were low. The weather was fine, the food good, the wine abundant and cheap.

So well did the Spanish tourist industry exploit the country's attractions that, starting in 1950, tourism grew into one of the mainstays of the economy in little more than a decade. The Mediterranean coastline became a ribbon of resort towns that could accommodate millions of visitors at the height of the summer season. In 1959, some four million foreign tourists visited Spain. By 1965, the number had risen to 14 million; by 1973, it had reached 34 million — approximately one vacationer for each Spaniard.

Over this period, income from tourists rocketed from $125 million to more than $3 billion, virtually wiping out Spain's huge trade deficit. And besides benefiting the country's balance of payments, tourism had major spin-off effects on the economy. To satisfy the growing needs of foreign visitors, the government developed projects to better roads, railways, water services, airports and public works. All along the eastern and southern coasts, the invasion of tourists was matched by an influx of Spanish workers who had been attracted away from their agricultural and fishing occupations to better-paid jobs in hotels, and in construction and transportation companies.

The drift from the countryside corresponded with a shift away from the rural values advocated by the Franco regime against those of urban Spain. In the 1940s, industrial districts such as Barcelona and Bilbao had been penalized for "treachery"; in the next decades, these areas were cosseted. The switch was first signaled in 1951, when the goal of economic self-sufficiency was quietly dropped, opening the way for the import of raw materials needed to fuel Spain's industries. In 1959, the corporatist ministers identified with the Falange were replaced by a group of technocrats identified with the Opus Dei movement. One of the technocrats'

Scores of day laborers, their mopeds parked haphazardly by the roadside, pick cotton on an estate near Seville. For centuries, such workers have been the poorest and most exploited in Spain; in the 1980s, despite government aid and attempts at land reform, they fared little better.

103

A mule-drawn cart laden with newly harvested grapes traverses the extensive vineyards of the Pedro Domecq sherry firm outside Jerez. The vines are planted in light-colored *albariza* (chalky soil), which retains water throughout the searing summer.

Picked grapes are laid out on round esparto grass mats to dry in the sun. The heat increases the sugar content of the grapes, which are dried for eight hours to two weeks before being pressed. The juice is then put in barrels to ferment.

Spain's most renowned drink, the fortified wine known as sherry, derives its name from the Andalusian town of Jerez de la Frontera, in whose environs it has been produced since the days of the Roman Empire. Fortified with distilled spirits, sherry comes in three principal styles — pale, dry *fino*, the rare *palo cortado* and the rich *oloroso* — and many intermediate blends, such as *amontillado*, a *fino* made mellow and dark by aging.

After the grapes — usually the white Palomino variety — have been picked, dried in the sun and pressed, they undergo two fermentations in barrels or tanks exposed to the air. This exposure causes a layer of yeasts, called the *flor* (flower), to develop on the surface in some casks. When this happens, the wine will acquire the distinctive, dry taste of *fino*.

Tasters give the wine an initial classification after it has been in casks for six months. The classification may change as the wine's flavor matures. The sherries are aged in huge, airy cellars, or bodegas, where the young wines are added to older wines of the same type to maintain a consistency of flavor, color and quality. Only sherry from the oldest, most matured casks is drawn off for blending and bottling.

In the 16th century, the best markets for sherry were the Netherlands and Britain. A stream of immigrants, many of British descent, settled in Jerez in the 18th and 19th centuries to found many of the houses that still dominate the business. The largest firm, Pedro Domecq, was established in 1730 by an Irishman; later it was built up by the aristocratic Domecq family from the French Pyrenees. By the 1980s, the company owned 5,800 acres of vineyards and 73 bodegas. The main markets are still abroad; 90 percent of all Spanish sherry is exported — 40 percent of it to Britain.

The manager of a Domecq wine cellar pours a sample of fermented wine into a glass with the aid of a *venencia* — a long-handled scoop designed to draw wine from the casks with minimal disturbance. This is the moment, six months after the grapes have been pressed, that the sherry is classified.

Casks of maturing sherry extend in all directions beneath the Moorish-style arches of a new bodega in Jerez. The sherry will be fortified with grape spirit or diluted alcohol and blended before reaching the consumer.

first acts was to remove quotas and other restrictions from about 50 percent of Spanish imports from the countries belonging to the EEC.

Much of the money to finance the imports came from abroad: the money emigrants sent home to families and the earnings generated by tourism. There was also a renewal of foreign investment, attracted by the low cost of Spanish labor, cooperative trade unions and the growing domestic market. During the 1960s, foreign investment rose from $156 million to $1 billion, most of that income coming from multinational companies in the United States, West Germany, France, Britain and Switzerland.

The most important means of mobilizing domestic investment funds, which still made up four fifths of the whole, was a system known as the "privileged circuits." Privately owned banks, which until the end of the 1970s controlled at least 40 percent of Spain's industry, were obliged to place a proportion of their deposits — amounting in some cases to more than 50 percent — with the Banco de España at nominal interest rates. This money was lent on very favorable terms to such "privileged" sectors of the economy as energy plants, shipbuilding companies and steel manufacturers. These industries had been earmarked by the authorities for special treatment.

The system scored a number of successes, but it was open to abuse. No controls existed over how money so lent was used. Often the number of companies entitled to cheap credit was too large for the available funds to be effective. The banks were also permitted to charge high interest rates to borrowers of the funds not allocated to the privileged circuits. As a result, many compa-

nies outside the sectors entitled to special treatment, even those in which the banks themselves had a stake, were undercapitalized.

The same haphazard approach characterized the workings of the INI, which remained the state's main instrument of industrial development. Among its achievements during the 1950s was the founding, in collaboration with the Italian firm of Fiat, of a national auto-manufacturing company, SEAT, whose 600 model was the first car owned by the majority of the population in Spain. The INI also got involved in promoting industrial development in depressed areas. By the time Franco died in 1975, the INI accounted for one sixth of industrial production, and it was a dominant force in such areas as coal mining, aerospace technology and chemical research.

But the INI had no autonomy. It was always subservient to the orders of government and thus was frequently used to bail out private concerns whose owners had connections in Madrid. It was also used as a fount of patronage by the administration. The boards of the various INI companies were treated as sinecures for the regime's supporters, especially members of the nation's armed forces. In 1978, when a new management team was brought in, it was discovered that more than half of the 4,000 directorships of INI companies were superfluous.

It was also typical of the piecemeal way in which the economy evolved that the INI was not responsible for the state's three lucrative monopolies: Telefónica (telephones), Tabacalera (tobacco) and Campsa (petroleum distribution). The government's holding in these businesses was managed by the Finance Ministry, which nevertheless

Thousands of olive trees grow in uniform lines across an undulating landscape in the Andalusian province of Jaén. Spain is the world's largest producer of olive oil, with an output of 658,000 tons in 1984-1985 — roughly 20 percent of the world total for that growing season.

adopted a passive role, allowing private stockholders on the boards and permitting them to run the companies. Such an arrangement fostered a close, sometimes incestuous, relationship between the administration and business, leading inevitably to corruption.

Despite these inconsistencies, the combination of domestic and foreign investment produced a remarkable industrial expansion during the 1960s. One of the benchmarks of the boom was the increase in steel production from two million tons to seven million tons, all of which was consumed domestically. Most of the steel was used for the renewal of industrial machinery, which was sadly outdated: A UNESCO report produced in 1958 had revealed that 58 percent of Spanish industry was still using pre-1920 equipment.

Spain's foreign trade reflected the changing nature of the economy. At the start of the boom, the country was spending a quarter of its import bill on foodstuffs, but within 10 years that share was down to 11 percent. Capital goods had replaced foodstuffs at the 25 percent level. The importance of agricultural exports underwent a comparable decline. In fact, the contribution of agriculture to Spain's gross domestic product almost halved during the "miracle" years from 1959 until 1973, when the oil crisis plunged Europe into recession.

Belatedly, Spain had joined the industrial nations of Europe, and in the process, it had undergone remarkable demographic changes. All through the boom years, the depopulation of the countryside continued at a redoubled pace. Some of the rural emigrés were estate workers displaced by the introduction of machines; the number of

tractors, for example, rose nearly six-fold between 1960 and 1972. Others were small farmers who, too poor to mechanize, decided to sell their properties; half a million farms disappeared between 1962 and 1972. Many more emigrés were young people who simply preferred the attractions of urban life. As a result of this high rate of internal migration, almost half the country's 50 provinces saw their populations decline at this time. Barcelona and Madrid, however, the two largest cities, continued to grow. They soon accounted for a quarter of Spain's population.

The result was nothing less than the transformation of Spanish society. The growth of industrial towns provided the conditions for the creation of a class of skilled employees, technicians, managers, administrators, salespeople and promoters, such as had never before existed on a large scale in Spain. Educa-

tional standards rapidly improved to provide the necessary training for the new workers. In 1964, only 5 percent of the labor force had secondary or technical education; by 1980, the figure was 24 percent. With higher qualifications and more job opportunities than ever before, the members of the newly expanded middle class were not only more numerous than their predecessors but also notably different in their lifestyles, attitudes and values.

Isabel Solanas — the surname is altered at her request — is in many ways typical of the new class. The youngest of four girls, she was born in Madrid at the end of the 1940s. Because her father had a secure government job, she did not suffer privations in her childhood. She remembers that "no one spoke of the Civil War with bitterness at home." After being educated at two private schools run by religious orders, she went to Madrid University to study philosophy and letters — then a common choice of female students. She left after two years, however, for it was 1968, the year of student revolt. Although she "threw a few stones when the police appeared on campus," she rarely went to classes because "the teachers were always on strike." Her father, fearing that his daughter might get mixed up in radical politics, helped her get a job as a translator for the Committee for Nuclear Energy — one of the organizations run by the INI.

This in itself was a sign of the times: In an earlier generation, Isabel might have been expected not to work but to marry. Under the Franco regime, a woman could take a job only if she obtained her husband's permission and presented a certificate of his approval to the employer. The type of job opportunity open to women was also limited.

Peasant women in the countryside labored ceaselessly; but in the cities, middle-class wives were expected to devote themselves to their homes and families. Only if they had time left over were they permitted to involve themselves in charity, education, health or other similar good works.

When Isabel took her first job, she had already met her future husband, Jorge — like her, from a comfortably off, conservative Madrid family. He was training to be a building cost estimator, and because they had little money it was six years before they married. They had a church wedding, for both are practicing Catholics. They have one daughter, Marta.

By the beginning of the 1970s, with Jorge working for a real estate agent and Isabel doing a secretarial job for an import-export firm, they were earning enough money first to rent, and later to buy, their present home, an apartment in one of the new residential developments in the southwest corner of Madrid. In this, they consider themselves fortunate, for private home ownership is not available to the majority of Spaniards. Mortgages are given only on terms of 10 years or less; they are difficult to obtain and never cover more than 50 percent of the purchase price of the property. The shortage of housing tends to encourage large households, continuing the tradition of the extended family among the working class. There may often be four breadwinners under one roof.

In contrast, Isabel, Jorge and their daughter have 1,500 square feet to themselves on the fourth floor of an 11-story building. Isabel employs a 17-year-old girl to look after Marta and to do the housework. The girl lives with the family and has one day a week free. Although the supply of workers for domestic service is on the decline, demand is as high as ever — not from wealthy, upper-class women or from large families, as was usual in the past, but from working wives and mothers. "I couldn't stand being in the house all day," Isabel says, "although I like cooking and things to do with the home."

Isabel pays the girl from her salary, another part of which is spent maintaining her Ford Fiesta. Jorge drives a Renault. Having two cars enables the couple to return home separately for lunch — still a common practice in Spain, partly because most people live close to their work, partly because in most homes there is still a housewife to prepare a meal and partly because the Spanish working day has traditionally incorporated a long lunch break. Isabel and Jorge make the effort because "it's about the only moment in the day when

In an Andalusian grove *(above)*, cork oaks stand stripped of their bark to reveal the bright orange trunks beneath. Once removed, the cork layer is taken by truck *(left)* to a processing factory in Catalonia, where it is made into wine-bottle stoppers for export to France and Germany.

In Cádiz, the chief export outlet for southern Spain, a crane swings a container onto a cargo ship docked behind its massive bulk. The port stands at the heart of a network of trade routes, handling such commodities as wine, sherry, salt, oranges, figs, cork and fish.

we're all together." They claim to have little leisure time, but they eat out at least two evenings a week, go jogging in the park on Sunday to combat the effects of their sedentary jobs and frequently organize weekend excursions with some of their friends.

Their greatest pleasure is travel. Like many people in their age and social group, they have been to England several times and enjoy London and the English way of life. This year, however, they will be vacationing in Spain. Their long-term ambition is to buy a vacation home, but for the time being, they content themselves with renting a weekend apartment in El Escorial, 45 miles north of Madrid, at the foot of the Guadarrama mountains.

The Solanas may not have everything they want, but as increasingly affluent members of the capital's middle class, they are not complaining. As Isabel says, "The truth is, we live very well. In fact, we've never really had any difficulties in life. Everything's gone very smoothly for us."

The economic well-being enjoyed by the Solanas household has not been achieved by many Spaniards in the years since the industrial boom ended. The rapid growth of the 1960s obscured three serious weaknesses of the economy: It was dependent on cheap energy, cheap credit and nonunionized, low-cost labor. The first flaw was brutally exposed in 1973, when the OPEC cartel sent oil prices sky high. Spain at that time was relying on imported energy for 70 percent of its needs. The OPEC price hikes immediately increased Spain's import bill by 25 percent; but while the rest of Europe adopted draconian policies to cut petroleum consumption, Spanish officials reacted with almost serene indifference. Believing that the price increases would be temporary, they trusted in their country's historic links with the Arab states to gain them special treatment. The uncertain leadership during the years of Franco's decline and the transition to democracy also delayed action. Energy-saving measures were not introduced until 1978, five years after the rest of Europe had taken action.

The complacency with which Spain greeted the oil crisis meant that no thought was given to trimming investments. In 1973 and 1974, both the public and private sectors embarked on ambitious projects for expansion in the aluminum, household-appliance, shipbuilding and textile industries. The shipyards were ready to consolidate Spain's position as one of the world's biggest shipbuilders. But the success of the yards had been based on the construction of tankers, and that market was about to collapse with the oil crisis.

The momentum of this investment strategy delayed for four years the recession that hit most industrialized countries in 1973. But when the slump did come in 1977, Spain was in a worse position than its neighbors. Government and business not only had failed to gauge the consequences of the energy crisis, they had also ignored the changing mood of the workers. Labor had ceased to be passive. The last years

A worker examines the hull of a tanker in a dry dock at Cádiz harbor. In the early 1970s, Spain ranked fourth among the world's shipbuilding powers; by the end of the decade the global oil recession had caused a rapid decline in the number of ships built and the number of orders taken.

of the Franco regime witnessed a growing militancy in the work force in the big cities. Although trade unions were banned, illegal organizations such as the Communist-controlled Confederation of Workers' Commissions and the socialist General Workers' Union had infiltrated the officially controlled labor syndicates. Strikes were frequent. The authorities sought to head off this militancy by conceding generous wage packages. As a result, a measure of peace was brought to the shop floor and labor costs increased sharply. Between 1974 and 1979, real earnings rose by 56 percent compared with a 6 percent rise in the United Kingdom and a 15 percent increase in West Germany. At long last, Spain had stopped being a low-wage economy.

The banks were badly affected by the recession because of their direct equity involvement in industry and because of a slump in the real estate market — another area in which they had invested heavily. The Banco de España was obliged to intervene to assist more than 25 institutions that had gotten themselves into difficulty. Some of the most illustrious names in the business succumbed, among them Banco Urquijo Unión, which had been in the forefront of Spain's modernization.

The most publicized collapse, however, extended well beyond the banks themselves. The Rumasa group, established by a sherry trader from Jerez, José María Ruiz Mateos, included a banking subsidiary that was the eighth-largest deposit holder in the country. Yet it represented only a small part of what had become, after 20 years of ac-

A harvest of dolls' heads — cellophaned, bald and bewigged — wait for the accompanying bodies at the Famosa doll factory in Onil village.

quisition, Spain's largest private holding company, with interests that embraced construction, hotels, insurance, luxury consumer goods, store chains and agribusiness. But Ruiz Mateos overextended himself in almost all of these areas, and in 1983, the González government was obliged to take the unusual step of expropriating the whole Rumasa group to prevent serious damage to the country's financial system. The Rumasa losses were subsequently found to amount to half the entire losses in the banking crisis.

For most Spaniards, however, the most serious aspect of the recession was mounting unemployment. The slowdown in the economy meant that for the first time since the 1960s, there was not enough work for first-time job seekers; and the parallel economic slowdown in northern Europe had removed the safety valve of emigration. By the end of the 1970s, the flow of Spaniards seeking work abroad had been halted and, as a result, the number of jobless within Spain's frontiers grew rapidly. The unemployment fig-

ure had risen from less than 150,000 — or 1 percent of the work force — before the energy crisis to 2.7 million, or 17 percent, in 1985.

Worst hit was the rural population, which accounted for 19 percent of the labor force in 1980 — less than half of what it had been in 1959, but still double the average of most European countries. The problem was most severe in the south, where the continued cultivation of crops requiring a great deal of care, such as olives, had encouraged families to remain on the land. In-

TOWNS THAT MAKE TOYS

Bringing fun to millions of children around the world is serious business for the three villages of Onil, Ibi and Castalla in Alicante province, centers of the Spanish toymaking industry. For almost a century, the villagers have provided skilled labor for the locality's principal source of employment.

A mainstay of production is the manufacture of plastic dolls, in which Spain has become a world leader. It pioneered the baby dolls of the 1950s and has since made teenage fashion dolls and plastic action figures with science-fiction themes. Despite such successes, the country faces competition from toymakers in the Far East, forcing firms to improve efficiency and quality.

In the factory, women workers sew clothes on the dolls. The toy industry sells 75 percent of its production to the domestic market; most of what is not sold domestically goes to countries within the EEC, especially France.

4

creasing mechanization, and the destruction of olive groves because of the consumption of other edible oils, put many southerners out of work. In the early 1980s, roughly 120,000 landless laborers in Andalusia and Estremadura were making ends meet only because of special-works employment, which provided them with a minimum four-day-week wage.

In the cities, too, unemployment rose more than tenfold. The statistics are confusing, however, for in the later years of the Franco era, a practice of holding more than one job at a time — *pluriempleo* — had become widespread. The habit was encouraged by Spanish working hours. Those employees on the so-called *horario intensivo,* or intensive shift, worked from eight in the morning until two or three in the afternoon without a break and then had the rest of the day off. This schedule meant that they were free to take on additional jobs in the afternoons and evenings.

The system of *pluriempleo* was prevalent among civil servants and the military — people who were poorly paid and who worked regular hours. Some professionals also used it to boost their income. For example, a Barcelona hematologist, Dr. Jorge Vilalta (not his real name), took a second job to support an expensive lifestyle on a salary that was not keeping pace with inflation. He supplemented his income as a full-time hospital doctor by working as a university lecturer in his free hours.

Born into a wealthy, landowning family, Dr. Vilalta is married with four children, two of whom are attending private schools. Although they live in an apartment that has a rent fixed at a relatively low level, he also owns a summer house inherited from his family, two cars and a BMW motorcycle. His

hospital income was increasing annually by an average of 7 percent, but he found his lifestyle squeezed at a time when prices were rising at more than double that rate. Consequently, he was happy to add to his earnings the 4,000 pesetas he could earn hourly by passing on his clinical expertise to students.

This arrangement, however, became illegal in 1984, when Spain's Socialist government passed the Law of Incompatibility. Intended to halt the abuses of the *pluriempleo* system among the professional classes, the measure stated that only those who had passed specific qualifying examinations could practice such professions as banking, teaching and accounting. After the law was passed, doctors could teach their medical specialties at a university only if they also qualified as trained academics. Even before the new legislation, there were signs that multiple employ-

ment was diminishing, partly because the increase in wages had lessened the need for it, but also because recession meant that there were fewer jobs.

In the case of Dr. Vilalta, the primary result of losing his secondary income has ironically been to force him to leave Spain's public-health system. He took a higher paying job with a private clinic — a step he took unwillingly because he supports the principle of a state-run medical service. The only alternative open to him, he believes, was a decline in the family's standard of living — a circumstance that he was not prepared to tolerate — or the old proposition of emigration, to take up a better-paid position in northern Europe.

The condition of Spanish workers has changed considerably since the end of the Nationalist regime. Franco encouraged a paternalistic kind of job security:

A concrete band of high-rise hotels overlooks the beach at Benidorm *(left)* on the Costa Blanca, a magnet for mass tourism. In contrast, the village of Calella de Palafrugell *(below)* on the northeast coast retains a quieter and more intimate charm.

Though wages remained low, jobs were for life, as long as a worker toed the accepted political line. It was extremely difficult to dismiss an employee unless the employer was prepared to pay generous sums in compensation. Since Franco's death, however, the liberalization of the economy, combined with the effects of recession, has made the business of hiring and firing much easier. It is only in the civil service that the jobs-for-life attitude still persists.

Much attention has been given to the protection of workers' interests. The 1978 constitution guarantees the right to strike and organize freely. Detailed measures governing wages, job security and work conditions are laid out in the Workers' Statute and the Basic Employment Law, both introduced in 1980. These measures make labor relations the joint responsibility of the trade unions and the employers (represented by the Confederation of Employers) instead of the government, as was the case before. In the initial euphoria of the return to democracy, both sides were willing to cooperate in an atmosphere of consensus formalized by the signature in 1977 of the Moncloa Pacts — mutual agreements covering economic, political and social affairs. In the context of labor, the pacts established a sort of social contract by which the trade unions agreed to moderate their actions and limit strike action in return for guaranteed wage increases to counter inflation. This spirit of give and take came under considerable strain in the 1980s, when both state and private businesses were obliged to cut their work forces during a time of severe recession.

Although Spanish workers are now theoretically well protected, in practice the exercise of their rights depends

On an Andalusian beach, a woman mends one of a pile of nets used by local fishermen, who trawl coastal waters for sardines, anchovies and mackerel.

largely on the strength of their union and the size of the company they work for. Union affiliation in general is limited. Although exact figures are hard to obtain, the government believes that no more than 20 percent of the country's nine million wage earners are dues-paying members. One reason for this weakness is the preponderance of small-size companies — two thirds of all registered firms in Spain employ fewer than 50 people. In these businesses the trade unions have limited influence and few members.

Whatever rights Spanish workers may be denied, the vacation is certainly not one of them: Spain recognizes 13 public holidays — as many as any other European country — and employees stretch these days off work into long weekends, called *puentes,* or bridges, whenever possible. Workers are entitled to an additional vacation allowance of one month, which is traditionally taken during August. As a result, some businesses and government offices in the cities come to a complete standstill at the height of summer.

The summer-vacation tradition is encouraged by the continuance of a practice, established by the Franco regime, of giving bonuses. Most workers are paid the equivalent of one month's extra pay in July, and the same sum is given again in December. A few firms even pay a 15th month's salary in the spring. Unions, however, have complained that employers tend to pay lower monthly wages to compensate for the bonuses; the system may eventually be phased out.

Although many of the problems associated with the transition to democracy were still unresolved, the Spanish economy entered a new phase in June 1985, when the treaty of accession to the European Economic Community was signed. Echoes of General Franco's protectionist philosophy remained on both sides of industry. To join the Community, Spain had to abolish its practice of levying import tariffs, an action that was seen by many Spaniards as more of a threat than an opportunity. Such sentiments were reinforced by a 1979 study that showed that 53 out of 94 leading Spanish industrial products would be adversely affected by Spain's membership in the EEC.

The prevailing opinion is that Spanish industry will need capital if it is to prosper in the free market. The country may need to rely even more on foreign investment and know-how. Much of the nation's manufacturing capacity was based on low-grade intermediate technology, and new up-to-date equipment and processes are needed urgently. But it does not seem likely that the funds and skills will be found locally; there is little sign in Spain of the kind of cooperation between universities and industry found in the United States and northern Europe.

Agriculture, on the other hand, was expected to reap immediate benefits from EEC membership, since farmers would have guaranteed markets and be protected to a much greater extent from competition with other non-EEC producers, such as Israel and the Maghreb countries. The benefits will not be uniform, however. Galicia's small-scale and highly uneconomic dairy industry, for instance, became superfluous when Spain joined the EEC. For any country, such adjustments are painful, but for Spain, standing at a political and social crossroads, the transition poses the greatest challenge since the economic miracle got under way. □

In Seville's Maria Luisa Park, pigeons cluster around an ornately tiled fountain for a refreshing bath. The graceful star-shaped pool, with its repeating border of ceramic flourishes, reflects Islamic design traditions that originated in Persia.

THE TILEMAKER'S ART

Photographs by Carlos Navajas

From the cloisters of Barcelona to the courtyards of Seville, sumptuous tilework ranks among the glories of Spanish architecture. The tradition began under the Moors, when Muslim craftsmen introduced the ceramic techniques and motifs of the Near and Middle East to embellish the palaces of the caliphs. Later, both Christian and Moorish artisans labored to add a distinctly Eastern splendor to the castles and cathedrals of Catholic Spain.

The early tilemakers decorated their wares by molding patterns in ridges and furrows on clay to hold richly colored glazes in place during firing. Renaissance workmen added delicacy and detail to the bold geometry of Arabic designs with a new method of painting directly on a fixative glaze. This process permitted elaborate murals to be commissioned by noblemen, wealthy merchants and guilds.

Today, the application of modern machine technology has made Spain the third-largest tile-manufacturing nation in the world. Yet some factories still employ the preindustrial methods of the Renaissance ceramists. Although their work is now likely to adorn shops, restaurants or private homes, they still look back proudly to a tradition that gave one of their 16th-century predecessors the lofty title of Master Tilemaker to the King.

Simple bouquets offered by the faithful contrast with an elaborately painted ceramic image of Our Lady of Hope on a wall plaque in Triana (*right*). Now a suburb of Seville, the town was the principal center of tile production in 15th-century Spain.

In a Seville ceramics factory, the work-
man on the left shapes tiles from wet
clay with a machine press. His co-
worker then stacks them for biscuit firing, an initial baking that dries the clay
in preparation for painting.

After the first firing, a craftswoman painstakingly brushes the tiles with a slip, or colored glaze, that will be hardened in a second and final baking in the kiln. Although the glazes appear pastel, the oven's temperature, rising as high as 1,800° F., will bring out deep, shining colors.

121

The designs on a selection of tiles spanning five centuries recall historical events, sell haircuts and lotions, even tell the time on a sundial.

122

Surrounded by floor-to-ceiling tiles advertising wine and spirits merchants, a solitary customer enjoys a drink and a newspaper in a Madrid café. Several tile-manufacturing companies still design and produce custom murals to meet clients' individual needs.

THE SOUL OF THE NATION

As light relief during a bullfight in the resort of Fuengirola, an aspiring torero — the son of the world-renowned El Cordobés — announces his presence to the bull. The sport continues to flourish in Spain, with 100 or more professional matadors fighting annually in about 500 corridas.

Few other Western European countries have a culture as instantly recognizable as that of Spain. The running of the bulls in Pamplona, the courtyard of the lions in the Alhambra Palace, the rattle of castanets, the swirl of a lace mantilla, what the French composer Claude Debussy described as "the deafening sounds of a guitar that laments in the night" — these things are unmistakably Spanish, symbols of an extraordinary culture that has its roots in the earliest civilizations of the Mediterranean. In Spain, moreover, the "high" culture of the royal court was always closely linked to the folk culture of the towns and peasant villages. Diego Velázquez, the great Spanish painter of royalty, also lavished his artistic talent on servants, tavern singers and water carriers. And Francisco Goya, though painter to a king, spent most of his time depicting the people and folklore of Spain — its festivals, dances, proverbs, superstitions; the disasters of war and the absurdities of politics.

Similarly, the music that Manuel de Falla composed for Sergei Diaghilev's Russian Ballet reverberates with the electrifying rhythms of the *jota*, an ancient folk dance of Aragon. By the same token, the best-known of modern Spanish poets, Federico García Lorca, sang of peasants, bullfighters and gypsy lovers; Pablo Picasso, the undisputed *maestro* of modern painting, borrowed some of his most dazzling ideas from the folk potters of Valencia, who have

been turning out unsigned masterpieces ever since the Bronze Age.

This enduring alliance between high culture and folk art can be found, too, in the principal characters of the most quintessentially Spanish of literary adventures, Miguel de Cervantes' *Don Quixote*. The novel's eponymous hero (the "Don" is an honorific, comparable to the English "Sir") represents the literate segment of Spanish society in 1600. He has read the medieval romances and feels entitled to a share in them; education, such as it is, has turned him into a dreamer and an idealist. His long-suffering servant Sancho is the earthy pragmatist who has sustained Spain through all its vicissitudes, though he and his master must often pay the price for Quixote's romantic misconceptions.

Together they ride through the desolate, red-earth landscape known as La Mancha, an improbable region that lies close to the center of Spain but is neither a province nor any other official territorial entity. It was to this inhospitable area that Cervantes was dispatched as a tax collector. Middle-aged at the time and the author of an unsuccessful novel and some unpublished plays, he had the reputation of being a ne'er-do-well, though he had served with distinction under the Spanish admiral Don Juan of Austria and had been wounded in action. His tax district included the famous windmills at Campo de Criptana, which gave rise to one of Don Quixote's most famous encounters, and to an argument between Sancho and his master that sums up the essence of their relationship:

"Take care, your worship," said Sancho, "those things over there are not giants but windmills, and what seem to be their arms are the sails, which are whirled round in the wind and make the millstone turn."

"It is quite clear," replied Don Quixote, "that you are not experienced in this matter of adventures. They are giants, and if you are afraid, go away and say your prayers, whilst I advance and engage them in fierce and unequal battle."

The first part of Cervantes' tale was published in 1605 and proved an instant success: Within a few years there were editions (mainly pirated) in Madrid, Valencia, Lisbon, Brussels, Milan, London and Paris. The second part was

published in 1615, but it made little difference to Cervantes' precarious financial situation: He died in Madrid, "old, a soldier, a gentleman and poor," on April 23, 1616. It was the same date as Shakespeare's death, but actually there was a discrepancy of 10 days because the English had not yet adopted the reformed Gregorian calendar.

Not the least of the typically Spanish qualities of *Don Quixote* is its profoundly critical and rebellious tone. The book used to be regarded as subversive, and though it was tolerated in the mother country, it was prohibited for centuries in Spain's American colonies, where any revolutionary tendencies were repressed with greater zeal than they were at home. Cervantes had made his central character a moon-struck dreamer, precisely because it took a madman to speak the truth in a land governed by the Inquisition; thanks to

his lunacy, Quixote enjoyed the almost total freedom of expression that has generally been denied the saner characters of Spanish literature. He dared to question the social order and make fun of established authority; he lampooned the book-burning and intellectual repression that took place under the Inquisition; he castigated the persecution and expulsion of the Moriscos — Christian converts who were descended from the Moors.

Don Quixote remains the most-prized work in an era of masterpieces: the so-called Siglo de Oro (Golden Century) of Spanish literature, which in fact lasted nearly 200 years — from about 1500 to the 1680s. It was a period of dazzling achievement: In addition to *Don Quixote,* the Siglo de Oro produced a succession of classics in poetry, fiction, drama and social criticism by such writers as Lope de Vega, Gracián, Calderón, Luis de Góngora, Tirso de Molina and Quevedo. Many of these authors, like Cervantes himself, had trouble with the censors: Some of Quevedo's most incisive works circulated only in manuscript copies because they had not been approved.

Lope de Vega, who established the three-act comedy as the definitive form of Spanish drama, also created the prototype of the dashing, defiant man of letters: He served time in prison for writing scurrilous verse, and he irritated the authorities with his propensity for becoming romantically involved with women above his station. A master of sonnets, ballads and songs, he wrote with a prodigious facility and turned out more than 500 plays, making him the most prolific dramatist of the epoch. A friend with whom he agreed to collaborate on a play asked Lope one morning how he was progressing. "I

In the village of Almagro in Castile-La Mancha, actors rehearse a play on the stage of an open-air theater known as the Corral de Comedias. Dating from the 17th century, the playhouse is the only one of its period to survive in Spain. It specializes in productions of classical Spanish drama.

got up at five," Lope reported, "finished the act, breakfasted, wrote an epistle of fifty tercets, and have now finished watering the garden, and a rather tough business it has been."

The Siglo de Oro has its counterpart in Spanish painting, whose Golden Age is generally held to have coincided roughly with the 17th century. An unsentimental approach, whose special quality has been defined by the English writer V. S. Pritchett as "dramatic psychological realism," is characteristic of the best works of the time. Its great artists were, in his words, "brilliant intellectual observers, more penetrating than affective or sympathetic." The sense of distance between painter and subject is a notable characteristic of even El Greco, the earliest and most atypical of the Spanish Baroque masters, in pictures such as his famous *Burial of Count Orgaz* or the *Martyrdom of Saint Maurice,* with their cool colors and gaunt, elongated figures. El Greco, meaning "the Greek," was not, of course, Spanish by birth. His real name was Domenikos Theotokopoulos, and he was born in Crete in the middle of the 16th century. He studied painting in Venice and Rome before going to Toledo, then one of the main centers of Spanish painting, sculpture and architecture. Though his art failed to please Philip II, who banished the *Saint Maurice* altarpiece to the Chapter Room of the Escorial, El Greco was to become extremely popular with the Toledan nobility, whose portraits he painted with great insight and authority. Their long and aristocratic faces appear even in the most mystical of his religious pictures; the *Burial of Count Orgaz* has a whole row of them among the onlookers — an example of realism combined with visionary religious ecstasy.

Velázquez was the culminating figure of Spanish 17th-century painting, and also the most acute observer of his time. A native of Seville, he began painting folk subjects, such as his *Old Woman Cooking Eggs,* as soon as he finished his apprenticeship and opened his own studio, in 1618. He was called to Madrid five years later and there became court painter to Philip IV. Velázquez repaid his royal patron with a magnificent series of 82 portraits of Philip, his queen and their children.

In one of his most famous paintings, *Las Meninas (The Maids of Honor),* of 1656 or 1657, he combined the royal family and their retainers in an astonishingly fresh and unprecedented way: The little princess, five- or six-year-old Infanta Margarita, is surrounded by her court ladies, a dwarf companion and a pet dog; older women and a court

THE MASTERPIECE OF THE MOORS

Like dwellings throughout the Islamic world, the Alhambra hides its beauties behind stark, forbidding walls and towers.

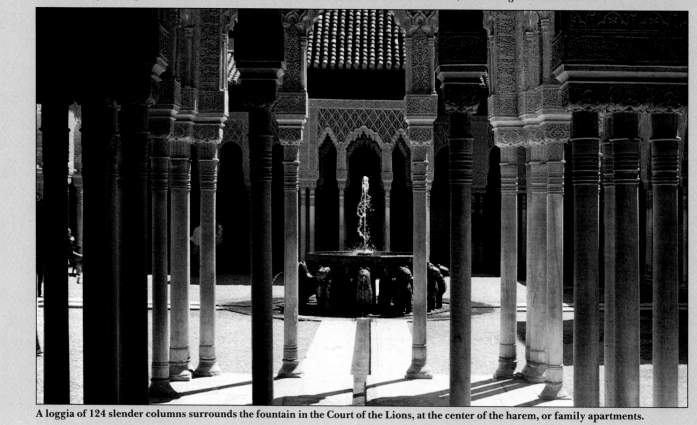

A loggia of 124 slender columns surrounds the fountain in the Court of the Lions, at the center of the harem, or family apartments.

Of all the buildings the Moors left behind them in Spain, not one rivals the Alhambra in Granada for beauty. The Arab kingdom that was ruled from this city remained an enclave of Muslim culture almost to the end of the 15th century, some 200 years after the rest of the Moors' Spanish empire had been recaptured by the Christians. When Ferdinand and Isabella's armies took the capital in 1492, the Catholic monarchs were so entranced by the palace there that they made it their own residence and chose it as their burial place.

Built largely of the russet bricks that give it its name — *al hambra* is Arabic for "red" — the residence dates almost entirely from the 15th century. No effort was spared to make it beguiling, with scented gardens, cool, tiled courts and splashing fountains. Running water, fed by the snows of the Sierra Nevada, was used throughout as an integral design feature.

The Alhambra is the only medieval Arab palace to survive intact anywhere, but it was not until 1870, after centuries of neglect, that it was declared a national monument. Today, its meticulously restored courts are busier than ever, echoing the footsteps of a million visitors each year.

official appear in the background. But the canvas also shows Velázquez himself in the process of painting another picture, his palette and paintbrush in his hands; behind him, in a mirror on the wall, we can see the subject to which his gaze is directed — not the little princess, but the king and queen. Besides being a superb character study of faces and personalities, the whole ensemble is an almost miraculous game of images-within-images, like the theatrical play-within-a-play. And no one but the inimitable Velázquez could have carried it off using members of the haughtiest royal family in Christendom as his models.

Francisco Zurbarán, a year older than Velázquez, excelled at painting another vital aspect of Spanish life — the various orders of monks in their monasteries. Among his favorite models were the White Friars, whose robes he painted in stark planes and shadows that emphasized the geometry of the folds and captured the shades of ivory and gold reflected in them. Toward the end of his career, Zurbarán's dominance of painting in Seville was challenged by the young Bartolomé Murillo, a painter who had great charm and ability but lacked Zurbarán's sense of composition. Significantly, Murillo's three styles have been labeled, consecutively, cold, warm and vaporous: In the hands of his innumerable imitators, the "vaporous" manner led Spanish painting into a sentimentality from which, for a time, there seemed to be no escape.

Yet, a century after the Siglo de Oro, just as the arts seemed becalmed in effeteness, Francisco de Goya y Lucientes breathed new life into them with his vibrant paintings of people from all walks of life — beggars, kings, peasants,

A prodigal use of sinuous patterns typifies the decoration of the royal baths.

At the age of 80 — after a lifetime of international notoriety — painter Salvador Dalí relaxes at his home in his native Catalonia. During the 1920s, Dalí gained fame in Paris as the most consciously outrageous artist of the Surrealist movement.

dandies, bullfighters, duchesses. A critical, rationalist spirit entered painting with Goya, who became the great painter not only of Spanish customs but of the Spanish psyche. Perhaps it was not entirely a coincidence that this remarkable rationalist was admitted to the Spanish Academy of Fine Arts in 1780, the year before the last victim of the Inquisition was burned at the stake. (A deist schoolteacher, Cayetano Ripoll, was sentenced to be burned alive for heresy at Valencia as late as 1827. However, Ripoll's sentence was ameliorated at the very last minute and he was hanged instead.)

Under normal circumstances, Goya might have enjoyed the quiet, good life of a court painter, but these were not ordinary times. Goya was witness to the passing of the old order and to the Napoleonic Wars that followed, plunging Spain into the terrible years of bloodlet-

ting, which he documented in one of the most dramatic indictments of inhumanity ever put on paper, *The Disasters of War*. In these etchings there are no heroes, only victims. The end of the war liberated Spain from Napoleon but brought back the Inquisition, along with the old monarchy, thus preventing Goya from publishing the *Disasters*. Another series of etchings, *Los Disparates* — 22 of his most satirical views of an absurd society — were also left unpublished for more than 50 years. By then, Goya had gone into exile and had died in Bordeaux. A drawing he made at the age of 81, just before his death, shows an old man with white hair and a beard walking out of the darkness into the light. His annotation in the margin reads: "I continue to learn."

The closing decades of the 19th century brought with them a threefold revival in other aspects of Spanish cultur-

al life — literature, architecture and serious music. The opening notes of this renaissance were sounded by Gustavo Adolfo Bécquer, a lyric poet in the German Romantic tradition who died a poor man in 1870: Most of his works were not published until after his death. At about the same time, Benito Pérez Galdos, a writer from the Canary Islands working in Madrid, published a Spanish translation of *Pickwick Papers*, and soon followed it with a series of novels that established him as a sort of Spanish Dickens or Flaubert — and perhaps as the greatest Spanish storyteller after Cervantes. His finest work, *Fortunata y Jacinta* (1886-1887), is a compelling study of the contrasts between marriage and illicit passion — the two women of the title are an affluent gentleman's mistress and wife, respectively. Millions of modern Spaniards were glued to their sets when it was adapted for television in the 1970s.

After Spain's demoralizing defeat in the Spanish-American War, a group of writers known as the Generation of '98 began to look inward and to discover the forgotten virtues of Old Castile: its stoicism, energy and courage. Among them were some of the most important literary figures of the last 100 years, including Pío Baroja, Azorín (José Martínez Ruiz), Antonio Machado, Miguel de Unamuno, Ramón María del Valle-Inclán, Jacinto Benavente and a resident Nicaraguan poet, Rubén Darío. They were followed almost 30 years later by the so-called Generation of 1927, which included the Nobel Prize winners Vincente Aleixandre and Juan Ramón Jiménez, as well as the essayist José Ortega y Gasset and the poet García Lorca — a group soon to be destroyed by the Civil War.

In the meantime, Barcelona had become a thriving cultural capital in its own right. The artists and writers of Catalonia no longer perceived themselves as provincials, living far from the intellectual centers of prominence. A new creative ferment was at work in all the arts, from poetry to design. The Catalan literary revival, called the Renaixença, had raised people's awareness of their separate cultural identity. It was succeeded by a startling architectural revival led by the most gifted, imaginative architect of the entire art nouveau movement in Europe, Antonio Gaudí, who created a one-man revolution in building design.

Perhaps more than any other visual phenomenon, Gaudí's buildings reflect the Catalan desire to possess a culture that is demonstrably different from that of Castilian Spain. Gaudí began designing houses in a quasi-Moorish style but soon evolved a brilliantly unconventional vocabulary of his own, using curves, arches, cupolas, columns, turrets, ramps, buttresses, undulating façades — a previously unknown amalgam of natural shapes and geometric forms. For Gaudí, moreover, the surfaces were no less important than the underlying structure, and he took almost unimaginable pains with the ornamental details of his buildings, which he had executed by all the skilled craftsmen then still available in Catalonia — master blacksmiths to execute his designs in wrought iron, master ceramicists and tilemakers, stone masons, wood carvers, makers of stained-glass windows and others.

With their help, Gaudí produced a stunning series of churches, palaces, schools, homes and apartment buildings, even a whole factory community. His Park Güell, with its kaleidoscopic colors and cavelike recesses, turned the

In his villa on the French Riviera, Pablo Picasso stands surrounded by a sampling from the vast range of his 75 years of artistic endeavor. Picasso left Spain for France when he was 24 years old, but Spanish themes, such as bullfights and guitars, recurred in his work until his death in 1973.

5

steep slope of one of the foothills skirting Barcelona into the most innovative public environment since the Hanging Gardens of Babylon.

At the turn of the century, Gaudí's Barcelona was a city of painters, poets and musicians busily creating an exciting art-nouveau culture that was linked far more closely to Paris than Madrid. Their headquarters was a café, beer-garden, cabaret and art gallery all in one, known as the 4 Gats. With a nod in the direction of the famous Chat Noir cabaret in Paris, it took its name from the popular saying "We're only four cats" — the Catalan equivalent of "There's nobody here but us chickens." Among the 4 Gats regulars were the painter-humorist Santiago Rusiñol, the art critic Miguel Utrillo (who later, in Paris, gave his name to Suzanne Valadon's illegitimate son, a gifted child who grew up to become the painter Maurice Utrillo), the portraitist Ramón Casas, the landscape painter Joaquín Mir and the young Pablo Ruiz Picasso, who, though born in Málaga, was a Barcelonan by adoption.

The 1901, Picasso made his first trip to Paris, where he settled permanently in 1904 and began, in his casual, almost insolent way, to revolutionize modern art. Still, he often returned to Spain: The fragmentations of cubism were developed not only in Paris but in a village called Horta de Ebro, near Tarragona.

And although Picasso became world-famous as the ageless *enfant terrible* of French modernism, he never relinquished his Spanish passport or his spiritual ties with Spain; it was only Franco's victory in 1939 that made him decide never to set foot on his native soil again. At the outbreak of the Civil War he went to the defense of the republic with a cycle of etchings, *Sueño y Mentira de Franco (Dream and Lie of Franco)*, which was like an updated version of Goya's *The Disasters of War*. Then, when Franco's German planes bombed the ancient Basque capital of Guernica, Picasso responded with the fierce, anguished mural that is the most famous image to come out of the conflict. After years in safekeeping at the Museum of Modern Art in New York, it was finally repatriated to Spain in 1981 — 42 years after the war's end — in token of the fact that democracy had been restored and, ideologically, the war was at last over. Two other famous Spanish painters who were active in France, Salvador Dalí, and Joan Miró, had come home by then and spent the last decades of their lives on native soil; Dalí on the Costa Brava, Miró in Majorca.

Picasso's long and immensely productive life — from 1881 to 1973 — was a one-man recapitulation of everything that had happened in Spanish art for the past 10,000 years. He reached back to the paintings of Altamira Cave for the bulls of his *Tauromaquía*, to Celto-Iberian pottery for his own sculptures and ceramics, to the narrative style and vivid coloring of the medieval *Cántigas de Santa María* of Alfonso the Wise for some of his paintings, drawings and lithographs. The screaming horse of *Guernica* is a direct lineal descendant of the horses in the 10th-century illustrations of the famous *Commentary on the Apocalypse* by Beatus of Liébana, which warns of the imminent destruction of the world.

Picasso had broken with the academic tradition in which he was raised, yet he knew and revered the great masters of the Spanish Baroque. One extraordinary series of 58 Picasso oil paintings is devoted to paraphrases and metamorphoses of Velázquez's *Las Meninas*. He donated the entire series to the Picasso Museum in Barcelona — a vast collection of his works that had been assembled by Catalan friends in the 1960s. It is housed in the medieval palace of Berenguer de Aguilar, in the Calle Moncada, which runs through one of the city's oldest quarters. This splendid subtreasury of Picasso's work contains hundreds of representative paintings, from the earliest to the last of his many periods, magnificently displayed against ancient brick arches and the clean-scrubbed stone walls of a palace built between the 13th and 15th centuries.

Appropriately enough, it was Picasso who designed — and also painted — the decor and costumes for the finest Spanish ballet of the 20th century, *El Sombrero de Tres Picos (The Three-Cornered Hat)*, which Diaghilev commissioned from Manuel de Falla when his Russian ballet company took refuge in neutral Spain during World War I. Picasso gave it a drop curtain depicting a bull ring, executed in a style reminiscent of Goya's tapestry cartoons; Falla composed his electrifying music based on folk rhythms, and Leonid Massine, the choreographer, learned the steps from a flamenco dancer named Félix, who was taken into the company as a supernumerary for the purpose.

The great renaissance that took place in Spanish music around the turn of the century was the work not only of Falla but of Isaac Albéniz, the virtuoso pianist who composed the brilliant *Iberia* suite, and of Enrique Granados, and gentle, lyrical composer of songs, piano pieces and the opera *Goyescas*, based on scenes from Goya. But Albéniz died of Bright's disease at the age of 48, in 1909, and Granados was killed at the same age in 1916, while returning from the premiere of *Goyescas* at New York's Metropolitan Opera: The ship on which he was crossing the English Channel, the *Sussex*, was torpedoed by a German submarine. Only Falla was left to carry on the revival.

The Cádiz-born Falla was a shy and unassuming figure, "a man even smaller than myself," as his friend Igor Stravinsky noted, "and as modest and withdrawn as an oyster." Yet his music is full of fire. Falla's early scores, such as *El Amor Brujo (The Phantom Lover)* and *Nights in the Gardens of Spain*, managed to capture the essence of *cante jondo*, the "deep song" of the Andalusian gypsies. In later scores he turned dissonant and neoclassical. He set an episode from *Don Quixote* to neo-Renaissance music and composed a *Concerto for Harpsichord* that took its cue from such 18th-century masters as Antonio Soler and his Italian-born teacher, Domenico Scarlatti, who had been harpsichordist for many years to the Spanish royal family. The Civil War broke out while Falla was working on a major choral cantata, *Atlántida,* which was based on texts by the Catalan poet Jacinto Verdaguer. Falla was named honorary president of the Spanish Institute, founded by Franco, but he left Spain as soon as he was able to — in 1939 — and spent the rest of his life in rural Argentina. The *Atlántida* was never finished.

133

5

A crane rises behind the 330-foot-tall spires of Barcelona's unique Sagrada Familia Church *(below)*, designed by the architect Antonio Gaudí. The building was begun in 1882, but Gaudí constantly revised the plans until his death in 1926; today, work still continues on its unfinished shell *(right)*.

Throughout his life, Falla was an aficionado of *cante jondo* as well as a connoisseur of early music. In 1922, he and the young poet García Lorca organized a historic *cante jondo* festival in Granada, where both were then living; it was held in the Plaza de los Aljibes in the Alhambra. Both of them felt that *cante jondo* was being threatened by commercialism, and that the best way to keep it alive was to give prizes to those performers who were maintaining the true values of this ancient art.

The list of performers was headed by many of the foremost professional flamenco artists. Yet, the 1,000-peseta "Zuloaga prize" for the best flamenco singer was carried off by an unknown old man from an outlying village who had everyone sitting on the edge of their seats. His name was Diego Bermúdez, but he was known as El Tenazas (The Pliers), and had a voice rather like a rusty iron gate. He sang his *cante jondo* couplets in what was described as "a loud whisper."

This was, as Falla and Lorca well knew, the heart and soul of flamenco singing; untutored, spontaneous, yet ancient in its lineage. El Tenazas deserved the prize because, as the Spanish saying goes, he had *duende*, a word signifying spirit or passion. The *duende* is the guardian demon of the *cante jondo;* to say "this has much *duende*" is the highest praise. Lorca once gave a lecture on "The Theory and Function of the *Duende*," in which he explained that "the *duende* is a power and not a behavior," and he recalled what an old guitarist had told him: "The *duende* is not in the throat; it comes up through the soles of the feet."

Lorca came closer than any other writer to expressing in words the painful depth and bitter austerity of Spanish folk dance and folk music. He saw its power as a function of the imminence of mortality: "Spain has always been a nation open to death." Ironically, Lorca was to experience the literal truth of this terrible perception when, at the beginning of the Civil War, he was taken to the outskirts of Granada and fusilladed in an olive grove. His death has been explained as the personal vengeance of some of the Fascist bullies, whose wartime slogan was *Abajo la inteligencia; ¡viva la muerte!* — "Down with Intelligence; long live Death!"

For long, the memory of that fearful conflict cast a deep shadow over literary life. The Civil War deprived the nation of most of its writers and intellectuals, thousands of whom were killed or forced into exile. After several barren years, Camilo José Cela resuscitated the Spanish novel with *La Familia de Pascual Duarte,* published in 1942, which launched a tough new realism in fiction known as *tremendismo.* The book deals unsentimentally with the harsh and violent life of a peasant from Estremadura, who is executed as an assassin, though he is guilty of committing only a mercy killing. Some of Cela's subsequent novels examined other brutal aspects of the day-to-day existence of the poor. As he wrote in his introduction to *La Colmena,* which was set in a sordid Madrid café in 1943: "This novel of mine doesn't aspire to be anything more — nor anything less — than a piece of life told bit by bit, without reticence, without charity, as life goes, exactly as life flows by."

Despite the example of Cela, the situation of writing and writers in Spain remained precarious until the death of Franco. It was not until the advent of democracy that many new names arrived on the scene. The recent upsurge in publishing and intellectual activity as a whole has brought to prominence such writers as José Luis Sampedro, Juan Gil Albert, Rosa Chacel Francisco Ayala, Juan Benet, the Goytisolo brothers, Francisco Umbral and in particular Gonzalo Torrente Ballester. His trilogy of passion and social conflict in prewar Galicia, *Los Gozos y las sombras (Joys and Shadows),* is the latest work to win recognition as a potential classic — one of the seminal works of modern Spanish literature. Out of the crucible of literal exile, or the so-called inner emigration, these writers have forged a Spanish modernism that is new in its attitudes to reality, yet retains its links with the great tradition of satire, pessimism and psychological detachment. They tend to dwell on the ludicrous

and magical sides of human experience that allow their characters to lead identifiably "Spanish" lives even at a time when Spain is becoming increasingly Anglicized, Frenchified and Americanized.

These same tendencies recur in the most notable examples of Spanish film, from Juan Bardem's *Death of a Cyclist* to the work of Carlos Saura and Victor Erice, whose *Spirit of the Beehive* was an international success. The greatest of Spanish directors was Luis Buñuel (1900-1980), a thorn in the side of respectability who, in a sense, was the archetypal Spanish intellectual of the 20th century. He grew up with, and then rejected, the austere, deeply

Catholic ideal of Spanish culture symbolized by Philip II's Escorial palace-monastery in the Guadarrama hills. As a young man, he went to Paris, where he made two movies in collaboration with Salvador Dalí — *Un Chien Andalou* and *The Age of Gold* — which established him as the surrealist film maker par excellence. But he quarreled with his friends in the Surrealist movement: On returning to Spain in 1932, he made *Land Without Bread,* an impressive documentation of hunger and misery in one of the forgotten corners of Estremadura. It was banned by the government of the Republic. Yet, during the Civil War, Buñuel was sent to America to assist in the making of anti-Franco

films — which were never produced.

His Mexican period began with a thrilling portrait of the dregs of Mexican society, *Los Olvidados (The Forgotten Ones),* which won a prize at the Cannes Film Festival of 1950 and reestablished his reputation in Europe. During the 1950s, he worked mainly in France, making films about his multiple obsessions — religion, death, sex — using humor, cruelty and eroticism as weapons against any kinds of ideological or social conformity. In 1961, the Franco government adopted a cautious, open-door policy toward some of the prodigal sons of Spanish culture. Buñuel was invited to Spain to make a film of his own choosing, and the result

THE WORLD'S FASTEST BALL GAME

Glistening with exertion, a red-sashed pelota player prepares to fling the hard rubber ball toward the end wall of the court. The leverage provided by his two-foot-long *cesta*, or scoop, may propel the ball at speeds of more than 100 miles an hour.

Pelota — also known as jai alai — has spread through Spain and Latin America, but it is in its original home, the Basque Country, that it is seen at its fastest and most furious. The game is played on a concrete court, or *frontón,* that is about 33 feet wide and 165 feet long; one side is open, except for a screen to protect spectators. The players — one or two on a side — use wicker scoops to hurl the ball down the court so that it hits an end wall above a marked line. Opponents must then catch it on the rebound, before it bounces twice, and return it the same way. The speed and agility of the players combine with heavy betting — conducted by bookmakers who face the onlookers — to create a spectacle that is passionately involving for the initiated and highly exciting for the ordinary spectator.

was *Viridiana,* which won the Golden Palm award at the Cannes Film Festival but was denounced as blasphemous by spokesmen for the Catholic Church. The film was not allowed to be shown in Spain until 1977.

By then, Buñuel had made a whole series of key films abroad: *The Exterminating Angel, The Discreet Charm of the Bourgeoisie, The Phantom of Liberty* and *That Obscure Object of Desire.* In these, as in all his films, Buñuel remained loyal to one of the tenets of surrealism: the subversion of received wisdom and accepted values. He was not a political but a moral revolutionary: His criticism was directed against all the prescriptive and repressive forces of society. Conversely, he was fascinated by alienated beings who were somehow immune to moral censorship: beggars, cripples, prostitutes and all those who transgressed the conventional laws and standards. There is no trace of sentimentality in any of his films. It was said that Buñuel was the most universal of Spanish film makers — and also that he could have come from no other place than Spain.

Like the "high" culture it has so often enriched, Spain's popular, or folk, culture has endured difficult times to survive into the latter part of the 20th century. The main threat to it, however, has not come from above, in the form of a hostile officialdom, but from below, with the growing loss of its popular base to the seductions of the mass media. Ironically, this has happened at a time when folk traditions are more feted and honored than in any other period in Spanish history. Lorca's beloved *cante jondo,* for example, has now acquired world fame and professional status, similar to that enjoyed by the blues in the United States. The blues,

however, is black music, brought over from Africa with the slave ships and adapted to new conditions in the Old South, whereas *cante jondo* represents a survival of the oldest native music of Spain, sung by the people centuries before the gypsies — who have now adopted it — arrived in the land.

Over the years, however, the gypsies of southern Spain have become so closely identified with this ancient idiom that they have a virtual monopoly on certain kinds of singing, dancing and guitar-playing. The generic term for these is "flamenco," a word sometimes traced to Arabic sources, though its likelier derivation is from the Flemish courtiers and soldiers who came to Spain through the Hapsburg connection. In the underworld jargon of 18th-century Andalusia, someone called *flamenco* was a swaggerer; by contrast, the word *gitano,* meaning "gypsy," had negative overtones. Thus, when gypsy music came into its own as an identifiable style, it was called *flamenco,* both to escape the stigma of *gitano* and to indicate that its foremost practitioners were the most dazzling and defiant of the gypsy musicians.

The earliest flamenco singers dealt with subjects of immediate social concern — passion, prison, prostitution, robbery, revenge. But the forms multiplied so rapidly that by the end of the 19th century, there were 30 or 40 recognized subgroups of flamenco song. Some of them were associated with specific localities, such as the *malagueñas* of Málaga or the *granadinas* of Granada, while others had to do with certain occupations — the *caleseras* of the buggy-drivers, the *martinetes* of the gypsy blacksmiths, the *carceleras* of prisoners in jail. One of the most famous and enduring categories is the *saeta,* the "ar-

row of song," which gypsy spectators address to the images of Christ and the Virgin Mary that are carried in Holy Week processions through the streets of Andalusian cities.

Only the most serious of these forms qualify as *cante jondo.* But true "deep song" is too profoundly emotional to be cast before listeners who are not knowledgeable about the art. Lighter varieties of flamenco song are known as *cante chico,* and these relatively undemanding forms, often adulterated with pop elements, are usually presented to tourist audiences in the "flamenco restaurants" of contemporary Spain. The same slide toward commercialism has occurred in the field of flamenco guitar playing. Some of the world-famous flamenco guitarists know nothing whatever about the ancient and honorable art of improvising variations called *falsetas;* they merely play whatever comes into their heads.

Only flamenco dancing has come off largely unscathed by TV and Hollywood influences. It is still possible, not only in Andalusia but in cities like Madrid and Barcelona, to see authentic flamenco troupes whose dancing truly lives up to the wide-eyed description that the composer Emanuel Chabrier wrote in Seville a century ago: "Those eyes, those flowers in their lively hair, those shawls around their waists, those feet that keep on tapping their ever-changing rhythms, those quivering arms running down their supple bodies, and the wavy movements of their hands, those sparkling smiles and that marvelous Sevillian behind that goes on turning and turning while the rest of the body doesn't seem to move at all! *Olé, Olé!*"

In other regions of Spain, where local folk music has not had the benefit of

137

A PROUD TRADITION OF HORSEMANSHIP

The uniform of the school's riders — piped jackets, wide-brimmed hats, polka-dotted scarves — hang ready for use on the stable yard gates.

The state-funded Andalusian Riding School, housed in a palace in Jerez, was founded in 1973 by the sherry magnate Alvaro Domecq, but its origins are much older. It takes its inspiration from the famous Spanish Riding School of Vienna, founded by the Hapsburg rulers of Spain and Austria in the late 16th century and still in operation today. The horses used in the Austrian school were originally bred from Andalusian stock, and the Jerez horsemen ride the same intelligent and spirited animals. Like their Viennese counterparts, they practice *haute école* horsemanship and give weekly public demonstrations.

Riders chat in the stables during a moment of leisure.

Riders entering the display arena in single file doff their hats in salute to the audience.

commercial encouragement, the main reason for so much of its remaining alive is that everyone loves festivals and feast days, and these, in turn, require special kinds of traditional music and dance. As a result, though folklore has largely disappeared from the everyday lives of ordinary Spaniards, many of them preserve the old songs and dances the way they do their Sunday-best suits, bringing them out of storage for their festivals. Sometimes the traditional old folk costumes are taken out of mothballs too, to grace the occasion.

Innumerable Spanish communities, both large and small, continue to celebrate their annual *romería,* a combination of pilgrimage and picnic that brings large numbers of people to a traditional shrine or sanctuary, often in the mountains or the countryside. The most famous of these popular outings is the *romería del Rocío,* which takes place each year on the weekend of Whitsunday (Pentecost) at the shrine of the Señora del Rocío (Our Lady of the Dew) in the village of El Rocío, north of the mouth of the Guadalquivir.

It is preceded each year by the most spectacular event in the entire calendar of Spanish festivals — Holy Week in the towns and cities of Andalusia, particularly Seville, where the ancient traditions are cultivated more assiduously than elsewhere. For an entire week, gowned and hooded penitents belonging to the 52 *confradías* (confraternities) of Seville pass in procession through the city's narrow streets with ornate floats of the Virgin or Christ. Here, the gypsies sing their impassioned *saetas* amid crowds jostling for a better view of the sacred images. Finally, on Easter Sunday, all the floats are brought to the city's cathedral to be blessed.

The pageantry and fervor of the

5

celebration are a southern phenomenon. Northern Spain observes Holy Week, of course, but cannot compete with the south in the splendor of its festivals; hence wealthy Spaniards from the north become tourists in their own country and go to Andalusia when they want to celebrate Easter in all its traditional color and exuberance.

Still, all the other regions have local spectacles that are culturally important and that play to the Spanish love of theater. The small town of Elche near Alicante, for example, preserves one of the world's oldest continually performed miracle plays, the *Misterio de Elche,* which is staged annually on the 14th and 15th of August in the town's largest church, the Basílica de Santa María. The city of Valencia has made a tourist attraction of its ancient fire festival, the *fallas de Valencia,* at which several hundred lampoon figures — latter-day successors of the straw dummies that used to be burned at the time of the vernal equinox — go up in flames amid the roar and sizzle of fireworks. And in many churches across the water on the island of Majorca, the highlight of the midnight Mass on Christmas Eve is still the traditional "Song of the Sibilla," which is chanted by a boy soprano dressed for the occasion in the robes of a pagan Sybil. The text is not a Christmas carol but a dire prophecy of what will happen to evildoers when the day of the last judgment arrives.

The Catalans, needless to add, carefully cultivate their own cultural traditions. The most eye-catching and convivial of their folkways is the custom of dancing the *sardana:* In Barcelona, weather permitting, it is danced every Sunday afternoon in one of the city's main squares, and there are similar performances in scores of other Cata-

lan cities and towns, since the dance is regarded as an important symbol of regional autonomy. Depending on the size of the community, hundreds of people may participate in the *sardana,* forming themselves into a dozen or so dancing circles.

But among the innumerable folk customs still flourishing in modern Spain, the most extraordinary and idiosyncratic are those that have to do with bulls and bullfighting. The ritual of bullfighting in the Mediterranean is at least as old as Minoan civilization, and bull worship apparently came to Spain along with the cult of Aphrodite, as evidenced by the presence of the dove, sacred to the goddess, on bronze bulls' heads used in prehistoric Spanish cults.

Although the sport still survives in the south of France and in Portugal — where the bulls are not killed — only in Spain and some of the former Spanish colonies has it retained its ancient status as one of the great public spectacles. For centuries, some forms of bullfighting were considered the preserve of kings and noblemen: Charles V, for example, won the affection of his subjects by killing a bull with his own lance on the day of the birth of his son, later Philip II. It was not until the beginning of the 18th century that bullfighting became a profession for the matador, *diestro* or torero — all three terms are used to designate the occupation of the man who, in Bizet's *Carmen,* is mistakenly called "toreador," an obsolete word for bullfighters on horseback.

In any case, the *corrida de toros,* literally meaning "the running of the bulls," is not and never has been a sport in the usual sense, nor is it a no-holds-barred contest between man and beast of the sort that the gladiators fought in the

Members of the flamenco class at a dance studio in Seville echo their teacher's sinuous and energetic movements. Once limited to the gypsy communities of Andalusia, which remain its spiritual home, the flamenco style of dance has become increasingly popular throughout Spain.

141

Roman arena. Properly performed, the bullfight is a kind of ballet or a piece of theater, as magnificently costumed as a religious ceremony, in which the man is supposed to live and the bull must die in accordance with a highly stylized ritual.

To ensure that the rules are strictly adhered to, every bullfight is held under the watchful eye of a judge or "president," perhaps the governor of the province, assisted by a veterinarian and an expert adviser, who may well be a retired matador. The bullfight is one of the few spectacles in Spain that always begin scrupulously at the announced time. As a rule, a complete corrida involves three matadors, who take turns killing six fighting bulls bred by the same ranch. Each matador is attended by his assistants: the dart-wielding banderilleros, the mounted picadors and their assistants the *mono-sabios*, and the *areneros*, whose job is to clean and clear the arena. Together they form his crew, the cuadrilla. Before the fight begins, the three superbly costumed cuadrillas of the afternoon march slowly across the ring to the traditional music of the Spanish two-step, the *paso doble*, saluting the judge and greeting the crowd.

Each encounter is divided into three parts, or *tercios*, preceded by a kind of overture: As a signal for the beginning of each phase, the judge waves a white scarf and the trumpeter and drummer sound a fanfare. When the bull is released and charges into the ring, it is first played by assistants with capes, the *peones*, to enable the matador to judge its characteristics; then he himself will step into the arena and make a series of passes with the cape. The first of the main acts is performed by two picadors, whose function is to wound and weaken the bull with short-pointed pikes. The second phase sees three pairs of barbed darts decorated with colored streamers, the banderillas, placed in the bull's shoulders by fast-moving banderilleros, or sometimes by the matador himself.

At last the climax is reached: the *tercio de muerte*, or death phase. The matador takes up his sword and his small scarlet cape and walks to the judge's box to request formal permission to kill the bull. The skill, elegance and courage displayed in the passes establish his domination over the bull and determine his standing as a bullfighter. He has only 15 minutes in which to demonstrate his ability to work in daring proximity to the charging bull, and only five minutes to achieve the most dangerous and difficult part of the ritual—the moment of truth when, if all goes according to plan, the matador will go in over the horns and kill the bull with a well-placed thrust of his sword. But bullfights rarely go according to plan. If the matador's sword thrust fails to locate a vital organ and the bull is in danger of slowly and painfully bleeding to death, he must quickly put the animal out of its misery with a special long-handled dagger, which he plunges swiftly into its head.

When the bull is dead, it is dragged out of the arena by a team of mules moving at full gallop to the sound of a *paso doble*. If it was very brave, it is granted a last circuit of the ring. The judge then rewards the matador for his bravery by granting him one or two of the animal's ears—in special cases, the tail of the bull as well. But great bullfights are increasingly rare, and the eras of toreros like Belmonte, Manolete and El Cordobés are spoken of with nostalgia by the aficionados who make up the knowledgeable fraction of the vast crowds who attend the bullfights in modern Spain.

But the audience for bullfighting is on the decline, along with many other aspects of the nation's folk traditions. In place of the customary evening stroll known as the *paseo* or a visit to a café, people are more likely to go home to watch TV—a state monopoly, partly supported by advertising revenues, that has become the universal information medium of present-day Spain.

Television began remodeling Spanish folkways during the 1960s. When men first landed on the moon, there were small groups of peasants sitting around TV sets in the cafés of villages and small towns. Then, gradually, people in the humbler walks of life began buying their own sets. Many older people who were never taught to read and write—and thus have highly developed memories—have turned into walking encyclopedias of knowledge about the world, which they have absorbed from home screens. Where once their information was bounded by the city limits, they can now discourse at length about the Transamazonian Highway, social conditions in Sri Lanka or the fauna of the Galapagos.

The advent of color TV sets during the 1970s served to increase television's impact, and at about the same time, Francoism and the Church's grip on public morality came to an end. An occasional nude body was to be seen on Spanish screens—an unheard-of phenomenon in the prudish days of Franco. But even before the relaxing of Spanish moral codes, TV served as a giant funnel that fed cosmopolitan influences into what had been a culturally isolated nation. In lieu of the native *zar-*

zuela, a home-grown brew of Viennese operetta and Spanish high jinks that had been popular since the 17th century, audiences became accustomed to *My Fair Lady* and *West Side Story;* with the dialogue dubbed into Spanish but the songs left intact in their original Broadway English. *Dallas,* dubbed into Castilian, was an overwhelming favorite. (It was subsequently shown in Basque and Catalan as well, for the new regional channels.) The question "Who shot J.R.?" exercised the nation far longer and far more profoundly than the political mystery "Who blew up Admiral Carrero Blanco?"

Of course, deliberate attempts were made to prevent Spain from being swamped by such alien matter, much of which must have seemed like something from Mars to the villagers of the Pyrenees or the Picos de Europa. There were folklore programs and folk dance contests. A weekly series was copro-duced with the networks of Mexico, Argentina and the other Latin-American nations who make up the 300 million Spanish-speaking peoples of the Western world. Yet, despite bullfight programs, guitar recitals and flamenco dancing, TV coverage of the native muse could not really offset the flood of outside influences: Chicago gangsters, Hollywood boudoirs with ivory telephones, and extravagantly named cocktails instead of good, honest

143

5

A full house crowds an arena in Madrid to watch an afternoon bullfight. The events usually start at 4 o'clock or later. In most big cities there is a fight every Sunday during the season, which lasts from March to October.

sherry or the local brand of firewater known as *cazalla*.

Just as television has revolutionized the culture-quotient of the average Spaniard, so the post-Franco press has broadened his information base to an unprecedented extent. *El País,* the left-leaning daily founded in the 1970s as a Spanish *Le Monde,* has emerged as the nation's most often-quoted newspaper, and magazines such as *Tiempo* and *Cambio 16,* based on the *Time* model, give Spanish readers a depth of field that was wholly unavailable to them for 40 years. The new freedom of the press has at the same time spawned a vast range of "girlie" magazines, science-fiction publications, photo-romances and violent Westerns. Only the fine arts and intellectual subjects are under-represented and are left to struggle weakly on in thin magazines and journals that have to be subsidized by local authorities or the Ministry of Culture in order to survive.

With the coming of new ways, a generation gap has started to appear in Spanish life. Youth culture, which in the latter part of the Franco regime was strongly political, has lost much of its social concern since the coming of democracy. Now it is focused on rock music, and the Madrid scene alone claims more than 200 groups and innumerable discothéques. Now disillusionment is in style, and there is a noticeable impatience with the thought processes of those who grew up in the old pretelevision days; they are sometimes disparagingly referred to as *carrozas,* the word for antique, horse-drawn carriages. With growing unemployment among the young, drug abuse has become a serious problem. Here, as elsewhere in Spanish life, parallels with other industrially developed countries

are becoming increasingly evident.

One pastime that seems relatively ageless in its appeal is soccer, by far the most popular sport in Spain. Spanish clubs are said to be the world's biggest spenders when it comes to signing up international stars. The annual expenditure of some of the principal clubs has reached one billion pesetas, and they have been known to run up exorbitant deficits. The first division league consists of 18 teams; their season begins on the first Sunday in September and runs to the end of May. The league champion enters the European Cup finals. Both first and second division teams participate in the Copa del Rey, the "King's Cup" knockout competition, whose winner then plays in the European Cup-Winners' Cup.

During the Franco era, soccer matches were the only massive concentration of crowds permitted by the govern-

ment, which reasoned that if people were preoccupied with soccer, they would not concern themselves with politics. The famous team Real Madrid won the European Cup on several occasions and was thus able to present the favorable international image that Spain so desperately needed. For that reason, it was said to be the regime's favorite team — which did not prevent it from compiling a genuinely brilliant soccer record. More recently, Real Madrid's grandeur has been on the wane, but the team remains one of Spain's greatest and has supporters throughout the country.

F. C. Barcelona, on the other hand, compiled an only mediocre record but still became the rallying point for Catalan nationalism during the Franco years, when all other manifestations of regionalism had to go underground. Its stadium, one of the world's largest, attracted 100,000 supporters every other Sunday: They never ceased to believe that *this* year their valiant but unlucky team would win the championship. Though it regularly failed to do so, its fans were never really disappointed by its performance: The phrase, *el Barça és més que un club* (Barcelona is more than a soccer club), coined by a local journalist in the 1960s, summed up its unique social position.

Surprisingly, the fact that political passions can now find other outlets has not diminished the popularity of the teams: If anything, crowds are larger and more enthusiastic than ever. In the Basque Country, the emergence of two highly successful squads, Real Sociedad de San Sebastián and Athletic de Bilbao, has led to massive popular demonstrations which were, for once, not in protest against some act of political injustice but were simply in support of local soccer heroes.

Accordingly, while the means of expression may vary, there is still a distinct linkage between the old Spain and the new: Whenever fresh forms of culture and communication are developed, they too will surely be co-opted into the service of the old loyalties and traditions of Asturians and Galicians, Castilians, Basques and Catalans. The fighting bull will go on, in the flesh or on television, representing the culture of Spain — even if the day should come when the fight is shown in digitally programmed three dimensions. And Don Quixote, whether in comic-strip form or rebroadcast from a satellite, will continue to uphold the ideals of a proud and ancient, if somewhat unpredictable, nation: "They are giants, and if you are afraid, go away and say your prayers, whilst I advance and engage them in fierce and unequal battle." □

COPA DEL MUNDO DE FUTBOL ESPAÑA **82**

A PASSION FOR FIESTAS

Fiestas are a cherished and spectacular part of Spanish life. Almost every town holds at least one annual gathering, usually celebrated with processions and pilgrimages, fireworks and dancing. Most commemorate a local saint or miracle, but there are also holidays to give thanks for the harvest, deliverance from the Moors or the safe return of fishermen from the sea.

One of the most impressive celebrations is Semana Santa, or Holy Week — a time of devotion and pageantry observed throughout Spain, but nowhere more elaborately than in Seville. For the week before Easter, the normal life of the city is suspended. Celebrants make processions to the cathedral carrying richly decked statues representing Christ's Passion and death.

While the mood of Holy Week is solemnly religious, other festivities are occasions for having fun. One of the most exuberant is Valencia's fire festival, held each March, when hundreds of painstakingly constructed effigies are burned simultaneously in a conflagration costing millions of pesetas. But for sheer excitement, no festival can match the Fiesta of San Fermín in the Navarrese capital of Pamplona, in which hundreds of young men prove their courage by allowing fighting bulls to chase them through the streets.

Dressed in penitents' robes, members of one of Seville's 52 religious brotherhoods process toward the cathedral. Each brotherhood is attached to a local church and is composed of parishioners who organize the Holy Week celebrations and raise funds throughout the year.

A pirate figure representing speculation and a crocodile symbolizing the consumer society dominate a *falla* satirizing capitalism.

148

For a week in mid-March, more than 300 squares and crossroads in Valencia are decorated with giant sculptures called *falla* — a local word meaning "fire." A typical *falla* consists of one or two huge figures surrounded by life-size caricatures arranged in tableaux that often satirize contemporary events. Some *fallas* take a year to construct and are so large that they have to be lifted into place by crane; but except for one or two effigies, which are saved for a local museum, all go up in flames on the last night of the revels.

Flames consume a giant hand — the last remnant of a *falla* — during the incendiary final hour of the festival, which traces its origins to the annual burning-off of wood scraps and other rubbish by the town's carpenters. By the next morning, even the street where the *falla* stood will have been scrubbed clean, and the 800 specialists and 1,600 helpers who devoted much of their free time to building the sculptures will already be planning next year's elaborate, though short-lived, creations.

THE HAPPY PILGRIMAGE TO EL ROCÍO

For 51 weeks of the year, the tiny Andalusian village of El Rocío is virtually deserted. In the week before Pentecost, however, its streets are crowded with up to 100,000 pilgrims, many of them gypsies, who come to worship at a shrine to the Virgin Mary.

The highlights of the *romería del Rocío* are an open-air Mass and a blessing of the Virgin, but the mood is not solemn. *Romería* means "picnic" as well as "pilgrimage," and the celebrations include dancing and feasting.

On the final day of the festival, pilgrims strain to touch a statue of the Virgin known as Our Lady of the Dew. According to legend, the shrine of El Rocío was built on the spot where the statue — hidden to protect it from the Moors — was discovered by a hunter after the Christian reconquest.

On a dirt road leading to El Rocío, men on horseback escort a flower-bedecked caravan of gypsies. Nowadays, only a few pilgrims travel to the shrine in the traditional ox-drawn wagons; most of them make the journey on horseback or by tractor.

Clutching rolled-up newspapers, the only defense allowed them, young men scatter before the horns of a charging bull.

THE RUNNING OF THE BULLS IN PAMPLONA

At 8 a.m. each day between July 7 and 14, a rocket fired from Pamplona's town hall signals the start of the running of the bulls, the most dramatic spectacle of the city's Fiesta of San Fermín. As the rocket rises, about a dozen animals are freed from a pen to dash along a half-mile-long route to the bullring. Watched by more than 30,000 spectators, about 1,000 young men race ahead of the bulls, dodging their horns. Until this century, only cattlemen and butchers could take part, but now the event draws many others, including tourists.

A Pamplona street vendor sells the red scarves and berets traditionally worn by the bull runners and those who come to watch. For the participants, rules governing dress and behavior are strict: They must not wear unusual costumes or make gestures that might single them out for the bulls' attention.

A PLAYFUL RESTAGING OF THE BATTLE WITH THE MOORS

All over Spain there are festivals to celebrate the Christian reconquest, but the defeat of the Moors is of special significance to the people of Alcoy in the Valencia region, which was one of the last areas to be liberated. Each April, the town celebrates with a two-day spectacular. Called simply the Festival of Moors and Christians, it is a colorful costume drama with the two sides simulating warfare until, to the accompaniment of bells and fireworks, the Moors are symbolically driven out of the town.

Amateur actors in fanciful Moorish costume advance down a street in Alcoy to do mock battle with other townspeople who represent the Christians.

ACKNOWLEDGMENTS

The index for this book was prepared by Vicki Robinson. For their help in the preparation of this volume, the editors also wish to thank: El Arenal, Seville; Miss Blair, Banco de Bilbao, London; Mike Brown, London; Kate Cann, London; Caracolillo, Seville; Ceramicas Vilar, Manises, Valencia; Windsor Chorlton, London; Colegio San Agustin, Madrid; Jane Curry, London; Bodegas Pedro Domecq, Jerez; Escolania de Montserrat, Barcelona; Famosa, Onil, Alicante; Los Gallos, Seville; Gimeno Martínez, Manises, Valencia; Andrew Firth, Anita Fraser, Harveys, London; Iberia Airlines, London; El Jerezano, Jerez; Jayne Kidd, Surrey; Peter Kinsley, Magalas, France; Ana Kolkowska, London; Dr. Stella Lander, Glasgow University, Scotland; José Antonio López de Letona, Information Office, Spanish Embassy, London; Mensaque y Rodríguez, S.A., Seville; Hermanos Morao, Jerez; Wendy North, VCL, London; Robin Olson, London; David Palengat, Domecq UK, London; Geoffrey Parker, St. Andrews, Scotland; Sylvia Perrini, London; José Samora, Spanish Embassy Commercial Office, London; Library, Spanish Institute, London; Spanish National Tourist Office, London; Deborah Thompson, London.

PICTURE CREDITS

Credits from left to right are separated by semicolons, from top to bottom by dashes.

Cover: Hans Wiesenhofer, Vienna. Front endpaper: Map by Roger Stewart, London. Back endpaper: Digitized map by Creative Data, London.

1, 2,: © Flag Research Center, Winchester, Massachusetts. 6, 7: Tor Eigeland, Barcelona, digitized image by Creative Data, London. 8, 9: Hans Silvester from Rapho, Paris. 10, 11: Patrick Ward, London. 12, 13: Hans Wiesenhofer, Vienna, digitized image by Creative Data, London. 14, 15: Carlos Navajas, Madrid, digitized image by Creative Data, London. 16, 17: Rob Cousins from Susan Griggs Agency, London. 18: Patrick Ward, London. 19: Digitized image by Creative Data, London. 20-22: Carlos Navajas, Madrid. 24: Fred Grunfeld, Majorca, Spain. 25: Juergen Schmitt from The Image Bank, London. 26, 27: Comisión de Programación de Emisiones de Sellos y Demás Signos de Franqueo, Madrid. 28, 29: Carlos Navajas, Madrid. 30, 31: Martyn Goddard from Daily Telegraph Color Library, London. 32, 33: Carlos Navajas, Madrid. 35: Stephanie Maze from Woodfin Camp Inc., Washington, D.C. 37: Carlos Navajas, Madrid. 38, 39: Hans Silvester from Rapho, Paris. 40, 41: Carlos Navajas, Madrid; Hans Wiesenhofer, Vienna. 42, 43: José F. Poblete, Frankfurt. 44, 45: Stephanie Maze from Woodfin Camp Inc., Washington, D.C. 46: Jean-Guy Jules from Agence A.N.A., Paris. 47: Tor Eigeland from Susan Griggs Agency, London. 48, 49: David Bayliss from Rida Photo Library, Kingston-upon-Thames, Surrey, England; Carlos Navajas, Madrid. 50: Photograph from Giraudon, Paris. 52: Archivo Oronoz, Madrid. 53: Adrian Deere-Jones from Bruce Coleman Ltd., Uxbridge, England. 55: Museum of Catalonian Art, Barcelona, from the Werner Forman Archive, London. 56, 57: Peter Christopher, Toronto; Luis Castañeda from The Image Bank, London (2) — Luis Castañeda from The Image Bank, London; Hans Silvester from Rapho, Paris; Timothy Beddow from Camerapix Hutchison Library Ltd., London — Sybil Sassoon from Robert Harding Picture Library, London; Luis Castañeda from The Image Bank, London (2). 58: Painting by Berruguezze, courtesy Museo del Prado (National Museum of Painting and Sculpture), Madrid, from Archivo Oronoz, Madrid. 60: Archivo Oronoz, Madrid. 61: Kunsthistorisches Museum, Vienna. 62: Illumination of Babylon burning from *Commentary on the Apocalypse* by Beatus of Liebana, 1047, courtesy Biblioteca Nacional, Madrid, photograph by Werner Forman Archive, London; private collection, photograph by E. T. Archive, London. 63: Archivo Oronoz, Madrid; painting, 1602-1605, photograph authorized by El Patrimonio Nacional, from Archivo Oronoz, Madrid; Mary Evans Picture Library, London. 64: "McKinley versus Alfonso" from *Le Rire*, 1898, by C. Léandre, photograph from Mary Evans Picture Library, London; *Guernica* by Pablo Picasso, 1937, © DACS, London, 1985, photograph by Archivo Oronoz, Madrid. 66: Courtesy Museo del Prado from Archivo Oronoz, Madrid. 68, 69: *Fusilamiento 3 de Mayo*, courtesy Museo del Prado from Archivo Oronoz, Madrid. 71: BBC Hulton Picture Library, London. 72, 73: Collection Cinémathèque Française, Musée du Cinéma. 74, 75: The Photo Source, London (2) — Imperial War Museum, London. 76, 77: Popperfoto, London — BBC Hulton Picture Library, London; The Photo Source, London. 78, 79: The Photo Source, London; Associated Press Ltd., London. 80, 81: Carlos Navajas, Madrid. 83: Associated Press Ltd., London. 84, 85: Carlos Navajas, Madrid, digitized image by Creative Data, London. 86: Alon Reininger from CONTACT Press Images/Colorific!, London. 89: Willy Puchner, Vienna. 90: Jean-Guy Jules from Agence A.N.A., Paris — Harry Gruyaert from Magnum, Paris. 92: Juergen Schmitt from The Image Bank, London. 94-96: Carlos Navajas, Madrid. 97: Rob Cousins from Susan Griggs Agency, London. 98-101: Carlos Navajas, Madrid. 102: Alice Arndt, Princeton, New Jersey. 103: Hans Silvester from Rapho, Paris. 104: Hans Silvester from Rapho, Paris — Gérald Buthaud from Cosmos, Paris. 105: Carlos Navajas, Madrid. 106, 107: Herbert Fristedt, Sundbyberg, Sweden. 108: Carlos Navajas, Madrid. 109: Antonio Gusmão from Colorific!, London. 110-113: Carlos Navajas, Madrid. 114: The Financial Times/Robert Harding Picture Library, London. 115: Alan Clifton from Colorific!, London. 116, 117: Hans Wiesenhofer, Vienna. 118-123: Carlos Navajas, Madrid. 124, 125: Gérald Buthaud from Cosmos, Paris. 126: Carlos Navajas, Madrid. 127: BBC Hulton Picture Library, London. 128: Ted Funk from Rapho, Paris — Jacques Pavlovsky from Rapho, Paris. 129: Adam Woolfitt from Susan Griggs Agency, London. 130: Manel Armengol from Black Star/Colorific!, London. 131: © Arnold Newman, New York. 132-135: Carlos Navajas, Madrid. 136: Walter Schmitz from Bilderberg, Hamburg. 138, 139: Gérald Buthaud from Cosmos, Paris. 140, 141: Carlos Navajas, Madrid. 143: W. Stanley Matchett, Belfast. 144: Joseph Viesti from Agence A.N.A., Paris. 145: Joan Miró/S.P.A.M., Paris, from Agencia Zardoya, Barcelona. 146, 147: Hans Wiesenhofer, Vienna; Gérald Buthaud from Cosmos, Paris. 148, 149: David Simson, Bisley, Surrey, England. 150, 151: Hans Silvester from Rapho, Paris. 152, 153: Blaine Harrington, Bethel, Connecticut. 154, 155: Luis Castañeda from The Image Bank, London.

BIBLIOGRAPHY

BOOKS

Anuario El País 1985. Sociedad Anónima.

Anuario Estadístico 1983. Madrid: Instituto Nacional de Estadistica.

Baedeker's Spain, 2d edition. Basingstoke, England: The Automobile Association, 1981.

Berendsen, Anne, *Tiles: A General History.* London: Faber & Faber, 1967.

Borrow, George, *The Gypsies of Spain.* London: J. M. Dent & Sons, 1924.

Boyd, Alistair, *The Companion Guide to Madrid and Central Spain.* London: William Collins Sons, 1974.

Brenan, Gerald, *The Spanish Labyrinth.* Cambridge, England: Cambridge University Press, 1943.

Brett, Michael, *The Moors: Islam in the West.* London: Orbis Publishing, 1980.

Brown, Dale, and the Editors of Time-Life Books, *The World of Velázquez* (Time-Life Library of Art). New York: Time-Life Books, 1969.

Canton, Sánchez, *The Prado.* London: Thames & Hudson, 1973.

Carr, Raymond, *Modern Spain 1875-1980.* Oxford, England: Oxford University Press, 1980.

Carr, Raymond, and Juan Pablo Fusi, *Spain: Dictatorship to Democracy.* London: George Allen & Unwin, 1979.

Cela, Camilo José, *La Colmena.* Buenos Aires: Prologo, 1951.

Cervantes, Miguel de Saavedra, *Don Quixote.* Middlesex, England: Penguin, 1950.

Ellingham, Mark, and John Fisher, *The Rough Guide to Spain.* London: Routledge & Kegan Paul, 1983.

Encyclopaedia Britannica, 15th edition. Chicago: Encyclopaedia Britannica, 1974.

Fodor's Spain 1982. New York: McKay, 1981.

Fraser, Ronald, *Blood of Spain.* Middlesex, England: Penguin, 1981.

Freidel, Frank, *The Splendid Little War.* London: Gallery Press, 1960.

Gilmour, David, *The Transformation of Spain.*

Topsfield, Mass.: Merrimack Publications Circle, no date.

Graham, Robert, *Spain: Change of a Nation*. London: Michael Joseph, 1984.

Grierson, Edward, *King of Two Worlds: Philip II of Spain*. London: William Collins Sons, 1974.

Harrison, Joseph, *The Spanish Economy in the Twentieth Century*. Kent, England: Croom Helm, 1985.

Humble, Richard, and the Editors of Time-Life Books, *The Explorers* (The Seafarers series). Alexandria, Va.: Time-Life Books, 1978.

Jackson, Gabriel, *A Concise History of the Spanish Civil War*. London: Thames & Hudson, 1982.

Kamen, Henry, *Spain 1469-1714: A Society of Conflict*. Essex, England: Longman, 1983.

Kubler, George, and Martin Soria, *Art and Architecture in Spain and Portugal and Their American Dominions 1500 to 1800*. Middlesex, England: Penguin, 1959.

Lee, Laurie, *A Rose for Winter*. Middlesex, England: Penguin, 1971.

Luard, Nicholas, *Andalucía: A Portrait of Southern Spain*. London: Century, 1984.

McKendrick, Malveena, *A Concise History of Spain*. London: Cassell, 1972.

Maravall, José, *The Transition to Democracy in Spain*. London: Croom Helm, 1982.

Michener, James A., *Iberia*. New York: Random House, 1968.

Mintz, Jerome R., *The Anarchists of Casas Viejas*. Chicago: University of Chicago Press, 1982.

Mitchell, David, *The Spanish Civil War*. London: Granada Publishing, 1982.

Morris, Jan, *Spain*. Middlesex, England: Penguin, 1982.

Muller, Joseph-Émile, *Velázquez*. London: Thames & Hudson, London, 1976.

OECD Economic Surveys 1981-1982, Spain. Paris: Organization for Economic Cooperation and Development, 1982.

Orwell, George, *Homage to Catalonia*. London: Martin Secker & Warburg, 1938.

Palan, Josepi Frabre, *Picasso in Catalonia*. Secaucus, N.J., 1975.

Penrose, Roland, *Pablo Picasso: Four Themes*. London: The Folio Society, 1961.

Perceval, Michael, *The Spaniards: How They Live and Work*. Newton Abbot, England: David & Charles Ltd., 1972.

Preston, Paul, and Denis Smyth, *Spain, the EEC and NATO*. London: Routledge & Kegan Paul, 1984.

Pritchett, V. S., *The Spanish Temper*. London: The Hogarth Press, 1984.

Read, Jan, *The Catalans*. London: Faber & Faber, 1978.

Reay-Smith, John, *Living in Spain in the 80s*. London: Robert Hale, 1983.

Richler, Mordecai, *Images of Spain*. McClelland & Stewart, 1977.

Russell, P. E., ed., *Spain: A Companion to Spanish Studies*. London: Methuen, 1973.

Salas, Xavier de, *Goya*. London: Cassell, 1979.

Schickel, Richard, and the Editors of Time-Life Books, *The World of Goya* (Time-Life Library of Art). New York: Time-Life Books, 1968.

Seagrave, Sterling, and the Editors of Time-Life Books, *Soldiers of Fortune* (The Epic of Flight series). Alexandria, Va.: Time-Life Books, 1981.

Sitwell, Sacheverell, *Spain*. London: B. T. Batsford, 1975.

Sordo, Enrique, *Moorish Spain*. Paul Elek Productions, 1963.

Spanish Constitution 1978. Madrid: Documentación Administrativa, Presidencia del Gobierno, 1978.

Stierlin, Henri, *The Cultural History of Spain*. Aurum Press Ltd., 1984.

Stravinsky in Conversation with Robert Craft. London: Penguin, 1958.

Thomas, Hugh, *The Spanish Civil War*. Middlesex, England: Penguin, 1977.

Troutman, Philip, *El Greco*. London: Hamlyn, 1984.

Walker, Bryce, and the Editors of Time-Life Books, *The Armada* (The Seafarers series). Alexandria, Va.: Time-Life Books, 1981.

Ward, Philip, ed., *Oxford Companion to Spanish Literature*. Oxford, England: Oxford University Press, 1978.

Weissmüller, Alberto A., *Castles from the Heart of Spain*. London: Barrie & Rockliff, 1967.

Wertenbaker, Lael, and the Editors of Time-Life Books, *The World of Picasso* (Time-Life Library of Art). New York: Time-Life Books, 1967.

Wilson, Simon, *Salvador Dalí*. London: Tate Gallery Publications, 1980.

Wood, Peter, and the Editors of Time-Life Books, *The Spanish Main* (The Seafarers series). Alexandria, Va.: Time-Life Books, 1979.

PERIODICALS

"Acclaim in Spain." *Time*, November 15, 1982.

Aris, Stephen, "What More Do the Terrorists Want?" *Sunday Times Magazine*, January 13, 1985.

"A Break with Tradition." *Time*, October 8, 1984.

"A Coup Fails in Spain." *Time*, March 9, 1981.

Crossland, Susan, "The Young Man Bringing Spain Back into the Fold." *Sunday Times Magazine*, February 10, 1985.

"Curing the Spanish Disease." *Time*, April 23, 1984.

Day, Douglas, "The Flame That Will Not Be Quenched." *GEO*, July 1984.

Duncan, Andrew, "The Moors Return." *Telegraph Sunday Magazine*, January 23, 1983.

Dutton, Gavin, "An Uncertain Future for the Barbary Apes." *The Listener*, November 1, 1984.

"An Election-Eve Plot." *Time*, October 18, 1982.

"The Fading of Eurocommunism." *The Economist*, December 24, 1983.

Financial Times Surveys:
"Andalucía," November 23, 1983.
"Galicia," November 17, 1984.
"Spain," December 9, 1983.
"Spain," April 13, 1984.

Gerassi, John, "The Endless Battle of the Basques." *GEO*, November 1981.

"Gonzalez's Spain." *The Economist*, October 27, 1984.

Graham, Robert, "Living in the Shadow of a Coup." *Financial Times*, April 8, 1981.

"Guilty as Charged, Sort Of." *Time*, June 14, 1982.

"Jeremy Harris in Spain." *The Listener*, December 20-27, 1984.

Kaplan, Marion, "Iberia's Vintage River." *National Geographic*, October 1984.

"The Last of the Forefathers, Joan Miró: 1893-1983." *Time*, January 9, 1984.

Mather, Ian, "The Siege of Gibraltar is Over." *The Observer*, February 3, 1985.

Matthews, Roger, "Why Spanish Democracy is on the Brink." *Financial Times*, February 24, 1981.

"The Night of the Generals." *Newsweek*, March 9, 1981.

Peffer, Randall, "Spain's Country within a Country: Catalonia." *National Geographic*, January 1984.

Roberts, David, "When Nothing on Earth is Sacred." *GEO*, January 1985.

"Spain's Socialists on the Move." *Time*, October 25, 1982.

Spencer, Michael, "On the Exotic Shores of Morocco." *GEO*, January 1985.

The Times Special Report on Spain, May 2, 1985.

Wilsher, Peter, Stephen Aris, and Jon Swain, "Carlos Routs the Rebels." *The Sunday Times*, March 7, 1981.

INDEX

Time-Life Books Inc. offers a wide range of fine recordings, including a *Big Bands* series. For subscription information, call 1-800-621-7026 or write TIME-LIFE MUSIC, Time & Life Building, Chicago, Illinois 60611.

ATLANTIC OCEAN

CANTABRIAN SEA

• La Coruña

GALICIA

• Lugo

Oviedo • Gijón

ASTURIAS

Santiago
de Compestela

Miño

Leon •

Pontevedra

CASTILE-LEON

• Orense

• Vigo

Zamora Duero

Salamanca •

Áv

Tagus

PORTUGAL

• Cáceres

ESTREMADURA

• Badajoz

Córdoba

Guadalq

Seville •

Huelva •

ANDALUSIA

GULF OF CÁDIZ

• Jerez de la Frontera

• Cádiz

COSTA DE LA LUZ

• GIBRALTAR

STRAIT OF GIBRALTAR

Ceuta

PALMA

LANZAROTE

CANARY ISLANDS

TENERIFE

FUERTEVENTURA

• La Palmas
de Gran Canaria

GOMERA

HIERRO

GRAND CANARY

ATLANTIC OCEAN

MOROCCO